COLD CASE MEDIUM

KEVIN'S STORY

E K Alexander

A self-published title
Animal Dreaming Publishing
www.AnimalDreamingPublishing.com

Cold Case Medium – Kevin's Story

A self-published book produced with the help and support of
Animal Dreaming Publishing
PO Box 672
Samford Village
QLD 4520
Australia

publish@animaldreamingpublishing.com
AnimalDreamingPublishing.com
@animaldreamingpublishing
@AnimalDreamingPublishing

First published in 2024

ekalexander57@gmail.com

A catalogue record for this publication is available from the National Library of Australia.

ISBN 978-0-6458836-6-4

While, this story describes the process Elizabeth goes through to help the victims, it is a fictionalised account and in no way a portrayal of actual events. Any similarity to persons living or dead is purely coincidental.

The information in this book is intended for spiritual and emotional guidance only. It is not intended to replace medical advice or treatment.

This book is dedicated to my beautiful brother,
David. Thank you for being part of our lives.
It must have been hard putting up with four sisters.

You are always in our hearts.

Author's note

This story is based on E K Alexander's work as a cold case medium. She receives messages from murdered victims of unsolved true crimes and assists in finding their remains so they can be put to rest, their families can find closure, and in some instances, the perpetrators can be brought to justice.

Chapter One

Have you ever sat and really wondered about your childhood, the things you did, and the many avoidable situations that you found yourself in? Well, I did. I only wish it were possible to turn back time and change some of them. Hopefully, I would have had the sense not to have walked alone in this area when I did, when I was upset as I was on that day.

Daylight was fading, but I knew the pathway well and I thought I would be safe. How wrong could I have been? I was murdered by two thugs who, according to them, 'Were just out to have some fun'.

I was fourteen years old when they took my life. At times I wished I could have been happier about my life, but there were lots of things in it that I still loved. My name is Kevin Hughes. I was born in 1950 in Cheshire England, and I died in 1964.

I was born into a time where people were struggling to make ends meet, and the remnants of World War II were still all around us. Derelict buildings were everywhere you turned. But that did not stop any of us having a good time, in fact we would use the buildings as places to hide from our mates and they would spend ages trying to find us.

Times were extremely hard. Those with jobs were the lucky ones. I knew the only way for me to have a future and get on in life was to do my best at school. I was not the sharpest tool in the box, as my dad used to tell me often, but I always tried my best at most of the subjects. Overall, I enjoyed going to school.

Every day after school, weather permitting of course, I would meet up with my mates for a game of football on the local field. It became a ritual. Me and a few mates would start by strolling home from school getting into all sorts of mischief on our way, taking our time as though we still had hours of daylight left.

When I reached my house, I would burst through the back door, head straight for the kitchen, throw down my satchel, shout 'hello' to Mum and my little brother, Owen, ram a jam sandwich down my throat and drink a glass of milk, if there was any.

Then I would shout, 'Right, I'm off out to play footy with my mates, Mammy.' Sometimes I would call her Mammy as that's what she called my granny, who was Irish. 'I won't be too long.'

Her answer would always be, 'You better be back in time for your tea. You know what your dad's like if you're not here when he gets home from work, so you better not be late!' And just as I was about to shut the door, she would add, 'And don't get up to any mischief, do you hear me? And don't slam the—'

BANG

'... door.'

'No, I won't, Mammy. See you later.' Somehow after saying I wouldn't slam the door, I always did it anyway.

I didn't mean to; it must have driven her mad. Hearing her say the same thing always brought a smile to my face. Things would not have seemed right if one day she hadn't said it. Then I would run to my mate Richard's house, and we would head to the field to meet the others and play football.

My parents met years ago in Wales, which is where my dad, Gavin, was from. He was born in the Rhondda Valley which is a coal mining town, and according to my mum, Brenda, he had a very impoverished upbringing. He could only find work in the mines and worked there as a young boy and into being a young man, finishing up not long after they met.

Mum had gone on holiday to Wales with her friends one summer and my dad was having a few days holiday with his friends at the seaside. She once told me that she had fallen in love with him straight away, but it had not been the same for my dad as he'd had a bad break up with his girlfriend not long before.

Mum had said she thinks the woman's name was Catherine, but she was not certain. They had been together for just over a year, but in the end, Dad finished the relationship for reasons he would not say. He really was not ready for another relationship, but somehow Mum managed to win him over.

Mum once showed me some photos of her and Dad when they were younger. She thought he was the most handsome man she had ever seen. He was tall with dark hair, and about twenty-four when they met. Mum was quite short and pretty and she always made sure that she looked the absolute best that she could. She was twenty-two and worked as a receptionist at an import and export office. It was not too long after they met that dad moved to Cheshire to be with my mum.

My earliest happy memory is at about four years old. I remember us chatting and laughing and having fun together: Mum, Dad and my new baby brother, Owen. I loved my little brother so much; he was so cute. I remember the day Mum and Dad brought him home from the hospital and have loved him from that day on. But over time, the happy moments lessened, and everything began to change.

Fast forward to when I am fourteen and my parents are no longer the happy couple they once were.

My dad seemed to always be worried or sad about something, and not loving towards us or Mum. He was always angry or impatient. His behaviour would upset me and my brother. As for my mum, many times I would hear her in her bedroom crying at night, especially after the arguments between them had become more frequent.

Dad had also started drinking a lot and spending more and more time at the pub, wanting to be left alone when he came home. This made everything worse, because he spent money from his wage on drink, which led to the bills not getting paid, which was a huge worry for Mum.

One day I had been out playing football and when I got home, I walked in on my parents shouting and arguing. Straight away I got a load of abuse thrown at me, my dad shouting in my face that I was 'nothing but a waste of space' and 'a lazy swine' – normal turns of phrase he had started to hurl recently.

Then he would say it was about time I got a job. At fourteen the only job I could have got was a paper round or work at the local market. I began thinking that there must have been something that set off this change in him, it was as if he was turning his anger at himself onto us and blaming us for whatever it was.

Not long after this, I walked in on Mum crying in the kitchen, Dad was nowhere to be seen. I asked her what had happened, and it all came out. Mum told me now because she felt I was now old enough to understand these things. And I think she really needed someone to talk to.

Mum had visited the shops last week and two of her friends from work stood outside chatting. She went over to say hello. She knew they were talking about her, because when they saw her, they stopped talking and turned away, pretending they had not seen her.

She approached anyway, asking them what they were talking about. Eventually one of them told her. They had seen my dad with another woman. Mum asked where and when, and at first, they did not want to say, but then they said it was down near the canal a few days ago. They didn't know much, but they could hear the woman had a Welsh accent and while she was talking to my dad, she seemed very angry.

When she got home, Mum approached Dad about this other woman, suspecting it was his ex-girlfriend from Wales, the one he had just finished with when he and Mum first met over fourteen years ago. During the argument things went from bad to worse and he raised his hand to hit her across her face, stopping in mid-air as he realised what he was doing, and then he stormed out of the house to go to the pub.

I had never known my dad to do such a thing. I wondered what was going on for him to do something like that, especially to my Mum. My first reaction was to wrap my arms around her, to make her feel better.

I began to feel so much anger towards my dad and drew back. 'Where is he, Mammy, in the pub as usual?'

She looked up at me with tears streaming down her face. 'It's okay, Kevin, there's not much you can do about it, love. You would only make things worse, and now you know what happens when he gets into one of these moods. He gets so angry, and I become frightened of him. Please leave it alone, it will only make things worse for us.'

'But Mammy, I don't understand why he has started being like this towards us, and I don't like it. Please tell me what's going on.'

'If I tell you, Kevin, you have to promise me that you won't tell anybody, or I will be in serious trouble.'

'No, I won't, I promise.'

'Before Dad and I met, he had just finished with his girlfriend, she was also from Wales. Do you recall me telling you a while ago?'

Kevin nodded.

'Well, I think he has been seeing her again, apparently two of my workmates saw them at the canal together.'

Kevin was shocked, 'What do you mean? Are you telling me they meet often? Is he going to leave us? Tell him to get rid of her!'

'Calm down, Kevin. I wouldn't have told you if I thought you would react like this. The last thing I need is for you to not understand what I am saying. Now I think about it, there must be a reason why she has shown up again, and believe me, it will all come out in the end.'

Luckily, Owen was at my Gran's house and did not see any of it happen, so for this one time I let it go. For Mum's sake. Two weeks later, things had calmed down a little. Mum never really got any answers from Dad about this other woman, he just clammed up. But it was now at the point where they stopped talking to each other apart from when he wanted more bread and butter with his evening meal, or another mug of tea. I would always stay around in the house whenever I could, to make sure she was okay, and he was not threatening her in any way. I would not go out if he were there. I suppose she got some peace when he was at work during the day, giving her time to relax.

A couple more weeks had gone by when one Sunday afternoon after football, I was walking home with Richard. As we neared my house, I could hear Dad shouting and swearing from outside. It was bad. I turned to look at Richard, who was equally shocked.

'I think it's best if you go home now, Rich. 'I better see what's going on.'

But Richard would not go, he wanted to see if everything was all right before he went home, so we waited quietly outside the back door. Within seconds we heard Mum shouting back at Dad, the shouting getting louder and louder until Mum screamed, and then silence.

I looked at Richard; we were both terrified. I pushed open the back door to find Mum crying on the floor, a small gash on her cheek and one above her eye which was bleeding. The bruising was already starting to show.

Dad stood over her. He reeked of beer. I flew into a terrible rage and began hitting him as hard as I could, shouting at him to get out of here, leave us all alone, and to not come back. I could see by the look on his face that he wanted to lay into me. His body was taut, and his fists were clenched.

'Don't you dare touch him!' Mum shouted. 'Get out and don't come back. Clear off with your fancy woman and leave us all alone.'

Instead of hitting me, he looked at me his face full of rage, and told me to get back to where I had been, to stay out of his way. He turned me about and pushed me hard, towards the back door. I banged my head on the door handle and fell to the floor, and for a moment my vision blurred.

When I touched the spot a moment later, there was already a bump forming. My dad, without looking back, casually walked into the living room, as if nothing had happened. Mum then came over to comfort me.

After realising my bump was not too bad, I remembered Richard was still outside. If Dad saw him, he would be furious. I told him to go home as there was nothing he could do here, even though one look at me made him very concerned. Then I went to attend to Mum. Blood was pouring down her face from above her eye. I got a flannel and some antiseptic and bathed her cut then her swelling face, I put a dressing on the cut and made her a cup of tea. I put a band aid on mine too, just for good measure.

Mum took a few sips then asked me to walk her to her bedroom as she felt a little unsteady. I helped her into bed and covered her over. I was about to walk away and leave her to sleep, when a terrible thought came into my head. 'Maybe all the times that I had heard Mum crying could it have been because he had hit her, and maybe that was why she always used the excuse that she had a bad migraine and had to go to bed.' But Mum told me this was the first time, and I believed her as I had never seen her with any injuries until now.

Dad's drunken snores could be heard all through the house, but at least he wouldn't bother us again tonight. A few days later Granny told me that Dad's behaviour had changed a few months ago, and he had started getting very angry towards my mum. Maybe when I had heard her crying in bed, it could have just been that they had been arguing.

I realised with a shock I hadn't seen Owen. 'Mum, where's Owen?'

'He was here when your dad came home and knowing what kind of a mood your father was in, I sent him to Gran's house. Will you go and ask her if he can stay with her for the night?'

'I will do, Mum. Will you be, okay?'

'Yes, I will. Now be a good lad and do what I say.' With every word that came out of her mouth I could see the left side of her face swelling up, but at least the blood had stopped. By the time we had finished speaking she no longer looked like my mum, the mum that I loved so deeply. Another person had done this to her, the person that she had loved for many years, but that love has probably now gone forever.

Once Mum was comfortable, I ran to Gran's, which was just down the road from us.

When she opened the door she said, 'Oh, my Lord, what have you done!' and ushered me inside. 'Please don't tell me it's that father of yours hitting out with his fists! Is your mother alright?'

'Not really, Granny, he had a go at her too. She had a cut over her eye, and I think she's going to have a black eye tomorrow.'

'That bloody man! If he carries on like this, I am going to get the police onto him.'

'Granny, listen. She's sent me round to see if Owen is okay, and to ask if you would let him stay here with you for the night.'

'Yes, of course. I will bring him back in the morning. Now you best get of home and see to your mother, make sure she is alright.'

'I will do, Gran. Oh! Where is Owen? I'll go and say good-bye to him.'

Owen was in the back garden kicking a football around on his own. I told him Gran was having him for the night, and he was fine with that. 'Be a good boy for Granny, won't you? I will see you tomorrow.' Owen was growing up and getting so tall, he was ten years old now.

I kissed Gran goodbye and set off home. I really loved my Gran. She was so funny and cuddly, and we always knew that if there was a problem, Granny would do all she could to help. She was always there for us, and no matter what the situation was, she would be there to help. As her front door closed behind me, for some strange reason I decided to walk a different way home this time.

And that was my big mistake.

I found myself going the long way, across Bonfire Hill, delaying getting home, buying time to face what had occurred. I wanted to get my mind straight, and the long walk, in peace and quiet, would be help me to calm down and give Mum more time to rest. As I was walking, I was thinking deeply about today's events, thinking about how I could get us all away from Dad before things turned much worse. Deep down I knew there was nothing I could do; I was a child. How would I be able to help? I was so deep in thought that I didn't even see my friend Richard approach. He was right in front of me, blocking my path before I noticed.

'God, Kev, what's the matter with you, mate? You're in a right daydream, I shouted you twice.'

Snapping myself out of it, I said, 'Oh sorry, Rich, I didn't hear you.'

'I know you didn't. Are you still thinking about what happened before? How is your mum and your head?'

So, I told him the whole sorry story, about my dad being seen with another woman and taking his anger out on my mum and me. I know I told mum that I wouldn't tell anyone, but I needed to get it off my chest and Richard was my best mate.

'What are you going to do? This is not good, especially when he is hurting you and your mum.'

'It's okay, Rich. I'll be alright. Mum and Owen are my main concern; I don't know what to do about it all.'

Richard walked with me for a while along the pathway at Bonfire Hill, and we talked about why it had such a nickname, just to get away from the subject of what Dad had done. It probably had another name, but we didn't know it. We called it Bonfire Hill because we would celebrate and build bonfires on the 5th of November every year – bonfire night.

This was the date that a plot to blow up the London parliament was foiled, hence the celebration of its anniversary. We used to have a brilliant time; it was a community get together with fireworks, toffee apples and treacle toffee, and the parents would bake jacket potatoes in the fire.

Before long, Richard said he had to get going, he was on his way to the shop for his mum. I said goodbye, and continued walking. A few minutes later I saw two lads walking towards me. They seemed to be focused more on me rather than anything around them. They looked around twenty years old. I don't know why, but I felt very wary of them.

The taller one of the two, sported a tough-guy stance, strutting about, smoking a cigarette from the side of his mouth. He looked like a self-assured bad guy from the movies, like a gangster or cowboy. He was trying to look cool, but to me he looked stupid. Not that I would say that out loud.

The other one was shorter, seemed a bit more insecure. He appeared to look up to him, maybe he was the one that did as he was told. I had never seen them round here before. Ignoring my feelings, I continued like nothing was wrong. Everything around me was quiet, and the three of us were alone. The sun was setting, and dusk was beginning to fall.

As they got closer and closer, I smelled the familiar odour of drink, just like when Dad had been at the pub. They had both been drinking. Alarm bells were ringing in my head now. Every step I took, my heartbeat got faster. Should I turn and run? I told myself not to be silly and try to keep as calm as possible. Maybe if I didn't make a fuss ...

Soon they were right in front of me, grinning at me. As I tried to move aside, they would block me, then block me again. I politely asked them to move out of my way, but they laughed. I was shaking all over but tried to sound and look calm.

Then they started circling slowly around me, trying to intimidate me, each time they passed getting closer to my face. The taller one of the two took a swipe at me and my glasses fell to the floor, and every time they circled me again, they purposely stood on them again until they were broken beyond repair. I told them I wanted to get home, but they did not stop. They clearly thought it was fun to intimidate a person in this way.

Suddenly, from out of nowhere, the taller one held a pen knife up in front of my face. His face was right up against mine and I could really smell the foul stench of beer. Out of fright, I pushed him out of my way as hard as I could. He fell over and I ran. There was no way I was staying around to see the outcome of that.

They chased after me, throwing rocks and bottles or whatever they could find but I kept trying to outrun them. My mind was racing. How to escape?

I got off the pathway and into the nearby woods hoping I could find a place to hide until they went away. I could hear them both laughing loudly behind me.

The shorter one said, 'Look at him, he's like a scared little lamb going to slaughter.' Then, in a sarcastic tone, added, 'Go on, run, you better run for your life, mate.'

I ran in and out of the trees, for what seemed like ages, until I could no longer hear footsteps. Ducking down behind a huge tree, I rested to get my breath back, still listening for more footsteps or voices. I stayed there for a few minutes, and all was quiet apart from my heart thudding loudly in my chest. I had never heard it beat that loud before. It was so loud, I even thought they might hear it.

When I had settled down and was confident that I couldn't hear them, I stood up, holding on to the tree for comfort and not wanting to let go. It was almost completely dark now. The thought of staying any longer in the darkening forest was becoming as terrifying as being chased.

I came out from behind the tree walking as slowly and quietly as I could. I could hear nothing but the birds. I headed back towards the field, and as I neared the edge, I smelled cigarette smoke. Even though I couldn't see them, I knew it was them and they were there, somewhere.

I ran as fast as I could, and so did they in hot pursuit. They were right behind me, shouting and back to throwing rocks at me, laughing all the time as if all of this were a game. A rock hit me on my head, and I fell to the ground bleeding badly. When I tried to stand, I was dizzy and fell back down.

As I lay on the ground clutching my head, they kicked me repeatedly. I held my hands over my face to protect it, which left everywhere else open. I felt every kick they gave me; the pain was unbearable. One of them pushed his foot hard down onto my legs while the other one kicked hard into my right side. I could not breathe, but the worse kicks of all were to my head.

There came a moment where I thought if I moved into a different position, it might give me a chance to try to stand up, but I was wrong. All it did was allow them to push me onto my back. I knew I had made a big mistake.

'Why are you doing this,' I yelled through my hands, knowing that they would go for my face if I moved them.

They paused kicking for a moment and the tall one answered. 'Because we're bored and need a good laugh.'

I was shocked. I looked at him and said, mumbling, 'Okay, so you've had your fun. Now let me be on my way.' I tried to stand up, but the smaller one pushed me back down.

I hurt my back as I landed, I think I must have landed on a stone or something. The tall one put his foot on my chest, and I could feel the weight of it as he pushed hard. 'You're going nowhere, mate. Not until we're ready. What's your name?'

Spitting blood out of my mouth, I said, 'Kevin.' But he only became more agitated.

He knelt beside me and gripped my hair with one hand and pulled out the pen knife with the other. 'That's not what your name is. Don't lie to me. You're that kid from the pub last night, the thieving little sod that stole my wallet.'

I was struggling to get my words out. 'No, I'm not. You have got the wrong person. My name is Kevin, I'm only fourteen. What would I be doing outside a pub?'

The smaller guy said, 'Come on, Tom, leave him alone, you've had your fun now.'

Tom grabbed him by the scruff of his neck. 'You stupid

idiot. Don't tell me what to do. Don't you realise what you have done?'

'No, what?'

'You've said my name, so now he'll give it to the police.'

Fearing for my life, I said, 'No, I won't, I promise, I won't say anything to anybody. I promise, let me—'

My words were all in vain, he was not listening. He slid the knife into me, cutting my sentence short. Blood oozed from my stomach. The pain was even worse than where I had been kicked.

'Oh my God, what have you done?'

He stared down at me, knowing fully what he had done. I placed my hands over the wound, feeling the warm blood pouring out, pressing harder as if trying to stop it and stupidly thinking I could push it back in. All I could think about now was trying to get home to Mum, which I feared now I never would.

Without even looking at me, Tom plunged the knife into me again, only this time it was to finish me off. My whole body went numb. I stared up into the star-filled sky, realising I was probably not going to get back to see Mum and Owen. The thugs were both looking down at me now, a look of fear on the shorter one's face.

'Come on, run! You've killed him,' he said.

Tom stayed there, staring. 'Shut up, Simon. And if you don't, you will be next,' he said.

Tom looked like he was in shock. I felt a moment of surprise wondering why he would be in shock after such a deliberate act.

Within moments, they were gone. I tried to roll myself to one side, to get up, but I kept falling back down. Laying there, in the cold and dark, I strained to keep my eyes open. I wasn't feeling pain now, maybe my body had gone into shock. I felt cold, but very calm. I started thinking about getting home to Mum, about how she will make me feel better and know what to do. And with that thought, everything changed. I could feel myself lying there holding onto my stomach, but it was all somehow at a distance. I had never felt that way in my life. I could sense the blood pouring out of me and was vaguely aware of the pain my body was in, but it didn't seem to matter.

At this point, Owen came into my thoughts, and I began thinking about all the funny things that he used to say when he was tiny. Then I saw Mum's smiling face, and images of Dad chasing me and Owen around the garden when we were younger, before he became a different person.

Then my thoughts changed to more serious ones. 'I hope Mum is going to be okay, and Dad doesn't hit her anymore. I love her so much. I wonder what Owen will be when he grows up. I hope Mum and Dad fall in love again once Dad sorts out his anger. I love them all so much.' When I finally allowed my eyes to close, I could not feel any more pain.

Then suddenly a beautiful bright white tunnel of light appeared in front of me. It made me feel so calm and peaceful, as if it were made from pure love. It was like a giant healing chamber. I wondered if I was supposed to step into it and it would make me better. I wanted to sit up and walk into it, but something stopped me. Fear overtook me and I panicked. I jumped up from the ground looking around everywhere, yelling, 'Mam, Mammy! I don't know where I am, come and get me.'

I saw my body lying motionless on the ground, and I was a distance away from it. 'That can't be me, I'm here!'

When I turned around, I could still see the white light. Feeling calmer, I knew I wanted to go into it. Then reality set in. I finally understood I was dead. My body, which was once the vessel for my soul, was no longer needed. My soul was now free to do as it pleased.

I walked towards the beautiful white light and stopped. I could not go. My mum needed me, and I had to stay to make sure she did not come to any harm from my dad. I had decided that I was staying here on earth to protect her, and hopeful that one day my killers would also be punished for taking my life away from me.

After a while, the light slowly disappeared.

When a person dies, their spirit leaves their body and carries on. It is only the body that dies. The vessel, the outer covering that has given us a physical presence for as long as we have lived. I looked down at the empty shell that was once my body, but now, outside of it as a spirit without a physical form, I was unable to be seen. I was left there all alone.

As I contemplated what might happen to me now, Tom and Simon returned. It was now pitch black. I am not sure how much time had passed. I stood a couple of feet away and they did not have a clue that my spirit was close by.

They shone their torches over my body, wondering what to do. It seemed they had come back expecting me to be alive rather than dead. They stood arguing for a while, each blaming the other, when really, they were both to blame. After a while they calmed down and the discussion moved to where they should bury me.

'Let's get him into the woods quick before somebody comes,' Tom said.

They picked me up, which was strange to watch from afar, and carried my lifeless body into the trees. They walked further and further into the woods, knowing that the further they walked the better the chance of finding a good area to hide me. After a while, they came upon a rocky overhang, with a very steep drop. It was an extremely dangerous area if you weren't careful where you were stepping.

They lay my body on the ground as close to the edge as they could, then rolled me over and stood in silence, listening to my body hitting every rock as I fell, then hearing the dull thud as I landed at the bottom. After rolling me over the top of the ledge, my body was now broken in so many places that I no longer looked like the person I once was.

They climbed carefully down after me and pushed me in closer to the rocks. Using anything that they could find, they started to frantically scrape at the dirt to cover me, then they walked away and left me there in the cold and dark as they began to climb back up to the top of the rocks.

Once they reached the top, Tom turned to Simon. 'We will have to come back tomorrow to hide his body properly.' Then he added, 'If you ever breath a word of this to anybody, you will be joining him, so you had better keep your mouth shut.'

Tom grabbed Simon by the throat, his eyes wide and

threatening. 'Do you hear me? If you tell anyone, I will find you no matter where you are, and I will kill you.' He repeatedly pushed his fingers into Simon's chest. 'Got it?' he said.

All Simon could do was nod his head. He knew Tom meant every word.

The next day, they returned to finish what they had started. In the daylight everywhere was so much clearer, so they decided to look for a better place to hide my body. Eventually Tom saw what he thought was a perfect place. Three tall black rocks were a distance away, but not too far that they could not drag a body there, and they decided that is where I was going to end up, for what might just be eternity.

They had brought a small spade with them adequate to do the digging, and an old sheet to drag my body to its new burial site. After a couple of hours their evil deed was done, my body was buried, and they had not been seen by anyone.

Chapter Two

The next day when Gran arrived at Mum's house with Owen, she was shocked at the sight that stood before her. Mum's face was really swollen, and the bruising had come out around her eye. Mum knew that she had to put the previous day's beating to the back of her mind for the sake of my Gran and Owen, and didn't want to talk about it.

Owen took one look at the sight of his mum's swollen face and burst into tears. Mum tried to comfort him, explaining what had happened in a way that he could understand. But Owen was just 10 years old, and he did not understand the dreadful things that happen in life. To see his mum in that state was heartbreaking for him.

After comforting Mum and Owen, Gran suddenly realised that I wasn't there. She thought I was still in bed. 'Where's Kevin? Isn't he up yet?' Gran asked.

'What? What do you mean? I thought he had decided to stay with you. I went to bed and took some painkillers for my headache. I must have slept all night.' Mum raced up the stairs to my empty room. When she came down, she was pale and shaking.

'Oh my God, Mammy, he isn't there. Where can he be?'

'Where is that large excuse of a man you married? Where is he? He could be out looking for Kevin.' Gran was really getting angry. 'Get him found so that he can look for his son.' As an afterthought, she added, 'He's nothing but an idol drunken lazy lout.'

Dad was asleep on the living room couch; he had been there all night. Mum shook him until he woke up.

'What the hell do you think you are doing, woman? Have you gone mad?'

He must have noticed the frightened look on Mum's face. He also noticed the swelling from what he had done to her. Dad sat up.

'Kevin didn't come home last night,' she said, and burst into tears.

He stood up suddenly, the rage already building. 'What the hell are you talking about? What do you mean he's not come home?'

Gran burst into the living room and stood by Mum's side. 'Are you deaf, or totally stupid? She is trying to tell you that Kevin isn't here. He came to my house last night to make sure that Owen was all right because, thanks to you using my daughter as a punching bag, we had to get him away from you.' Looking back towards Owen, then returning her gaze to him, she said, 'You've probably traumatised both of your children for life.'

Dad was shocked. 'What do you mean? Are you saying that it's my fault?'

'Of course, it's your fault. Do you think she did this to herself?'

Dad looked at Mum and Gran and could not believe the person that he had become over the past year or so. 'Where's Owen now, is he okay?' he said.

Gran gestured towards the kitchen and before anyone could say anything else, he pushed past them to see Owen.

Owen sat crying at the kitchen table, looking up as his dad came in. 'Why have you hurt my mum? Go away from me. I don't like you anymore.'

Dad had tears in his eyes. He scooped Owen up and held him in his arms, holding him tight. He told him how sorry he was for what he had done to his mummy, and that he will never do it again.

After everything had calmed down, Gran made a cup of tea, and they sat down to talk about things rationally. Mum sat with Owen on her knee, and they talked about what might have happened to me. When Owen realised, I was missing, he began to cry.

Granny tried to console him. 'It's okay Owen, everything will be fine, Kevin will probably be home soon. Don't worry about him, he could walk back through that door at any minute.' Gran tried to reassure him, but it did not make much difference.

It was incredibly hard to watch the sadness and the pain that they were all suffering and not to be able to tell them that I was dead and where my body lay.

Mum and Dad left the house to search for me and Gran took care of Owen. They walked the streets for hours, going to every one of my friends' houses, to ask if they had seen me. They got to talk to everyone except Richard, who had been out at the time they called round. Some of my friends' parents even joined the search.

It was as if something in Dad had changed with my disappearance. Instead of being the drunken ill-mannered slob, as Gran liked to call him, he was now getting people together and working out which groups should look in certain places for me.

The day's search yielded no results, so Mum and Dad called the police. Mum was in such a state that she could hardly speak when they arrived a few hours later. Gran was with Owen, trying to console him and making endless cups of tea for everybody, while all the time saying, 'It's alright Owen, Kevin will be home soon, and he will be fine.' Gran only said this as she did not want to put Owen through any more upset.

The officers kept looking at Mum's face, the youngest of them asking if she was okay. Mum said she was and told them that she had had a fall. Out of shame, Dad stared at the table as she spoke, but he did not correct her. I could tell the police had seen it all before. The young one returned to questioning Mum about me, asking who my friends were, if this was routine, and finally asking for a photo to take with them. They said they would get a proper search together, but it would not begin till the next day as it would soon be dark. This did not go down very well.

Mum flew into a rage and told them it had to begin now. 'He can't stay out there in the cold and dark all on his own, he needs to be found straight away.'

The officer made a big mistake. He said, 'Kevin has probably not disappeared, he will be at a mate's house having a good time and not realised how late it was.'

Dad took a step towards the officer. Mum grabbed Dad's arm to pull him back from hitting him. It was as if Dad realised something by this action, at that very second. He looked at Mum, held her in his arms and began to cry in front of the officers. 'This is all my fault. I should not have behaved the way did. I have upset all of you and not had any thought for anyone but myself. I hope Kevin is all right and safe wherever he is, we must get him found as soon as possible.' He turned to the officers, his eyes filled with tears. 'Please bring him home to us as soon as you can.'

The police officer said he would do all that he could, and his partner nodded in agreement.

That night it heavily rained all night long, washing away all the footprints and bloodstains that were part of the events leading up to my death. The next day the officers called round to report. Mum had been eagerly waiting for them, as she had been unable to sleep all night. Officers had been searching all the surrounding areas, including house to house. The search went on for days with no results.

Mum and Dad began to think that there was not much hope left of finding me. Then, the police got lucky at an estate near Bonfire Hill. A woman rang in and said that her son had mentioned he had seen Kevin the day he had disappeared. They advised her detectives would come to speak to her son shortly, and they radioed into the station.

Two detectives called round to see the woman within the next couple of hours. They were both noticeably young, probably in their mid-twenties. She invited them in and in a loud, bellowing voice shouted, 'Richard, come downstairs will you, the police are here about Kevin Hughes. Come down please and talk to them about it.'

Richard appeared in the living room looking nervous. One of the detectives introduced himself. 'Hello, Richard, my name is Detective Brown, and this is my colleague, Detective Moore. We would like to know if there is anything you can tell us about the missing boy, Kevin Hughes.'

Richard stood looking at them, not really knowing what to say. It was obvious by his red-rimmed eyes and anxiousness that he had spent a lot of time crying and wondering where his best mate had gone.

'The thing is,' he said, 'I don't really have much to say as I wasn't with him very long, probably five minutes or so. I was going to the shop for my mum at the time, which I think was the same day that Kevin went missing. I am not sure.'

The detectives sat quietly while he told them what he knew.

'I saw him near Bonfire Hill. When I first saw him, he looked over at me but never said anything. He continued walking as if he was in a daydream. I caught up to him and I told him that I had been shouting at him, but he ignored me. It was then that I knew something was very wrong—'

The detective stopped him in his tracks. 'Wrong, in what way?'

'Umm, he didn't seem to be himself, he looked scared.'

The detectives looked at each other.

'When he looked at me, he looked as though he had been crying.' Richard fidgeted, unsure if he should say more.

The detectives looked at each other again, then encouraged him to continue.

'I was with him that day after school, we both walked back to his house, and he walked in on a fight between his mum and dad. His mum was crying and bleeding—'

Detective Brown cut him off. 'Sorry, lad, just a minute. You are saying that his dad had beaten his mother? Did you go into the house with Kevin and witness it?'

'No, Kev told me to wait outside the back door as his dad would have been even more annoyed if he had seen me there, and he had hit Kevin too. He had a gash on his—'

The detectives looked at each other again. 'Can you tell me of any other time that you know of that Kevin had been hurt?'

'No, he'd never said anything to any of us before about anything like that.'

Detective Moore was writing everything down.

'Then I asked him why he was walking home across Bonfire Hill, and he said he needed some time to think about what to do, and that was the long way round to his house.'

'Right, okay.' Detective Brown had a puzzled look on his face. 'So, he's never told you about his father being violent towards him and his mother before?'

'No, Kevin is a good mate. We meet with some other lads on the field to play footy, and he has never spoken about anything like that to me or any of the other lads.'

Detective Brown looked at his colleague, and then back to Richard. 'Do you think you could give me the names of your mates? I would like to talk to them too.'

Richard gave him the names.

'Thanks, for your help, Richard, we will look into things, and we might have to speak to you again.'

They thanked Richard's mum as she led them to the front door. The detectives agreed Kevin's father needed to be investigated. Their next stop was to see Mr Hughes, as they put it 'to have a little chat'.

The detectives were surprised at my dad's height when he answered the door. 'My name is Detective Brown. Good evening, sir, we would like a little chat with you if you don't mind.'

He invited them in. 'Have you got some news about Kevin? Time is dragging on and on.'

The detectives were also surprised at his calm manner when he spoke. 'We do have something. Kevin was seen over at Bonfire Hill on the evening of his disappearance. We were also told that Kevin was in state of upset.'

'Upset? What do you mean by upset?'

My mum chose this moment to walk into the room, her face still showing the signs of a healing cut and bruising around her eye. They shook hands and asked her to take a seat.

Mum was hopeful they had come to say they had found me. 'Have you found Kevin? Where is he?'

'No, Mrs Hughes, I am sorry, but we don't have any information for you yet. It's your husband that we need to speak to. We need to ask him a few questions.'

'Questions about what?' Mum said, beginning to get upset.

Detective Brown looked over to my dad. 'We have information that you assaulted Mrs Hughes and Kevin on the day he disappeared. Is this correct?'

Mum and Dad looked at each other, knowing the evidence was still visible on Mum's face. Dad admitted this was true, recalling that he had been drinking. They asked him to accompany them to the police station for questioning. The detectives stepped outside the front door and with my dad between them and led him to the awaiting vehicle.

Mum stood on the doorstep in disbelief. As if all of this was not bad enough for her to have to contend with, two so-called friends from her work happened to be walking past on the other side of the road, the same people that told her about the other woman. They looked straight across, clearly delighted to have even more gossip, only this time about my dad.

Seeing my dad getting into a police vehicle had the women and our other neighbours thinking my dad had killed me, and that really hurt, especially after seeing his remarkable turn around and all that he had become recently. It was at this moment I realised that he loved all of us deeply.

Dad was escorted to a small room at the police station for an interview. Once they were all seated, the detective looked at him straight in the eye and said, 'Right, Mr Hughes. Can you tell us what happened between you and Mrs Hughes, then everything from the day of Kevin's disappearance, right from the start?'

Dad knew straight away that it was not going to be any use denying things, he had to tell them everything. Taking a deep breath, he allowed his words to flow.

'I had been at the pub, and I obviously had drunk more than I should. When I got home, because of the drink, I lost my temper. I haven't had a drop since. I feel so ashamed to have to admit to that.'

But the officers were not convinced. 'So, you do this sort of thing to your wife often do you?'

'It was all over a stupid argument, and she wouldn't listen to me.'

'And what was the argument about then?'

'I would rather not say. It's personal.' This answer did not go down very well with the detectives.

'I think it would be in your best interest to answer the question, if I were you, then we can get on with finding your son.'

Dad thumped his fist on the table, anger clear in his red eyes. 'This has nothing to do with my son.'

'I think we will be the judge of that.'

The questions went on for about another hour, and Dad was gradually being worn down.

'We just want to know, Mr Hughes, what the event was that made you so angry, so we can see if it has anything to do with Kevin's disappearance.'

Dad sat there with his head in his hands, wishing this were all a dream. 'For God's sake, leave me alone, will you?'

Detective Brown looked at him and said, in a stern voice, 'No, I don't think so, Mr Hughes.'

Dad looked up, defeated, and he knew from that moment on that he had to tell them. Okay, okay I will tell you. There's this woman—'

Before he could say anything else, Detective Brown said, 'Oh, I see, it's like that is it?'

Dad snapped at him. 'No, it's not what you are thinking. This woman is someone I used to know many years ago, maybe twenty years ago or more, before I married Brenda. I knew her when I still lived in Wales. But the thing is, I reckon she has followed me here, to Cheshire. She could have come here months ago. I'm not certain about that either, I am just going off when I started getting messages left for me at work.'

'What is it that she wants from you?'

'I don't know. She has been sending me threatening messages. She's been getting people at my work to pass them on. I had to meet up with her to put a stop to it. She is trying to get money from me, saying I got her pregnant, but then she says that she lost it, and now she is threatening to hurt my wife. She keeps saying different things.'

Dad sighed. 'I have not seen her for about twenty years. She was always a bit strange, but not as bad as this. The woman is mad.'

The detectives were listening carefully to every word, beginning to think that he was telling the truth. 'So, what did you do about it?'

'I went to meet her down at the canal, so that we could talk, and hopefully put an end to it all.'

'What's this woman's name?'

'Catherine. Oh God, I can't even remember her surname. I had to stop seeing her, she became so paranoid, she also said that if I don't start paying her money, she is going to kill herself. I am sick of all her threats. All the stress she has caused me turned me to drink. I didn't know what to do about it.'

He put his head in his hands again, wishing it was all over. 'I could not imagine how all of this would hurt Brenda, that is why I have not told her about it. But her work colleagues saw the meeting and that's what brought on the arguments and led to me hitting her and Kevin. I want all of this to stop. Please bring Kevin home, back to us where he belongs.'

The detectives were now satisfied with what my dad had said and believed that my disappearance was nothing to do with him. Mum did not want to press charges either, so there was no reason to hold Dad any longer. They told him that if he continues to still get threats from this woman to let them know, and they will deal with it, and then they let him go.

Chapter Three

Once the detectives had questioned the rest of Kevin's friends and yielded little else, they realised they had to go further afield, and visited the proprietor at the local pub. The pub was busy, everyone talking and laughing and enjoying a drink, until they noticed the detectives. Then the atmosphere suddenly changed, and everything went quiet.

The proprietor was a large man named John with lots of thick grey hair, a moustache, and rosy cheeks.

'John, can you recall any kind of unusual incident around the time Kevin Hughes disappeared? You know, the young lad that went missing last week?' Detective Brown asked.

'Oh yes, I know who you mean. No sorry, not that I can recall, but most of the regulars in here now might have been here that night too, maybe they will know something.'

Everybody in the pub was listening.

One man stood up and approached the detective. 'I remember something. There was a bit of a scuffle that night.' He looked at John. 'Don't you remember? There was all that commotion going on outside, between those two lads that we hadn't seen before, and those youngsters from the estate.'

'Yes! There was. It was between them two, and about three or four young lads on push bikes. I think one of the older blokes was accusing one of the kids of stealing something from him.'

'Did this man attack any of the kids?' said Detective Brown.

'No, not as I know, but when I went out there, that gave the kids a chance to run for it. One of them shouted, "Come on, Rich, let's get out of here!" and that's the last I saw of them.'

Detective Brown was about to reply, when suddenly the man said, 'Oh, hang on, there was something else. I noticed a car parked nearby too.'

'What kind of car was it?'

'It was a light blue Morris Minor Countryman, I think. In fact, I know it was, as it was parked underneath the lamppost so I could see its colour clearly. I have never seen it around here before either. Maybe it belonged to one of the men.'

At last, the police now had something solid to work with.

In the office the next day, the two detectives set about checking out the information they had received. They were sure the name Rich was more than likely going to be Richard Marshall, the young lad they had spoken to about Kevin's disappearance.

They followed up some other leads on other cases then headed to Richard's house in time for him to be home from school. They arrived as Richard was walking down the street. The detectives noticed he looked as though he had not had a good day as they got out of the car to meet him at the garden gate. When he saw them, he looked quite startled. Richard asked them to come in and they went into the living room where his mum was sitting having a cup of tea. She too was quite shocked at seeing them.

Detective Brown said hello and asked her if it would be okay to ask Richard a few more questions with her present. She said they could.

Detective Brown turned his attention to Richard. 'Can you tell me if you and some of your mates were riding your bikes over near the pub a few nights ago? The night before Kevin disappeared?'

'Richard, what have I told you about hanging around near that pub? Richard's mother said. 'Didn't I tell you not to go near there?'

'It's okay, Mrs Marshall, we are just asking some questions.'

Mrs Marshall sat back, glaring at Richard.

Richard looked sheepishly at his mum. 'Yes, well, sort of.'

Mrs Marshall shot off another glare. Detective Brown encouraged Richard to continue.

'Me and my mates were all out for a ride and stopped over the road from the pub for a rest. We could see everybody at the pub that came in and out. Two blokes came outside carrying their drinks. They were heading over to the wall to sit on. One of them was staggering. He dropped something on the path but didn't seem to notice because they carried on walking. I rode over there and picked it up to give it to him'.

'What was it?'

'His wallet. When I tried giving it back to him, he went off his head, shouting at me, and saying that I had tried to steal it. He threatened to hit me, so I threw it at him, then we scarpered quickly.'

Detective Brown asked, 'Did you see a name on it, or hear one of them say a name?' Richard shook his head. 'I definitely didn't hear a name and I didn't see a name on the wallet as it was dark.'

Detective Brown asked what the men looked like, and Richard told them all he could remember, which was not a lot.

'Is there anything more you can tell us?'

Richard was deep in thought, then a look of realisation spread across his face. 'Oh yes! There was a car there that looked a bit unusual. It was a sort of minivan with wood on the sides. I'm not sure about the name of it, but it was light blue, I think. We'd never seen one like it.'

'Okay Richard, you have been very helpful. If you think of anything else that might help us, will you let us know?'

'Yes, I will do.'

Detective Brown looked down and smiled. 'And by the way, you and your friends stay away from that pub in future,' he said, mimicking Richard's mum.

Richard looked up with a smile on his face. 'We will do, don't you worry.' When the detectives left, Richard followed them out.

Detective Brown asked, 'Is there something else you would like to tell me?'

Richard was trying to hold back tears. 'Do you think

Kevin will be found soon? I miss him so much. We all do, even the lads at school miss him, and it's just not the same trying to play a game of footy without him. Things will never be the same again.'

Detective Brown, saw the hurt on his face and as a father himself, wanted to hold him, but of course that was not allowed. In a gentle voice, he said, 'We will do all we can to bring him back home, don't you worry.'

'Do you think he is still alive?'

'That is not really for us to say. All we can do is to keep searching and find more clues.'

'Thank you,' Richard said, and headed back inside.

As the police car left and he closed the door behind him, Richard remembered the two drunken men who had been walking towards them that night when Kevin went missing. But then his mother called out to him to tell him off about being at the pub and it slipped his mind, and then he totally forgot about them. They wouldn't be those guys anyway, would they?

Days rolled into weeks and there were no advances in Kevin's disappearance. Everyone was feeling helpless and did not know what to do next. Richard decided it was time to help in whatever way he could and headed back to Bonfire Hill after school one day with his footy mate, Bert. They looked around the hill, then headed towards the woods. There seemed to be a lot of broken glass around the pathway. It was all from broken beer bottles. They picked up the large pieces of glass to put them over to the far side of the field, so that nobody would cut themselves on it. As they picked up the pieces, Richard noticed that on some of the glass there was what looked like blood.

'Hey, Bert,' Richard shouted. 'Come look at this!'

Bert came over straight away.

'Take a look, Bert. It looks like blood, doesn't it.'

Bert took hold of the broken glass. 'It does, Rich. What do you think we should do about it?'

'I don't know. This does not make any sense. Why didn't the police notice it? Unless they did and it's not blood at all. Maybe we are wrong, but maybe we were right. Do you think we should keep hold of it, and take it to the police?'

Bert thought for a few seconds. 'The thing is the glass could have got there after the time that Kev went missing. We better leave it here, perhaps move it out of the way for now.'

The boys decided to split up. Richard headed into the woods, and Bert went further towards the road. After a few minutes, Bert was shouting out waving something in the air, looking overly excited.

'Richard, look what I have found. I think I've found Kevin's glasses,' Bert said.

They ran towards each other and huddled together to get a closer look.

'One side of the frame is cracked like his were, and the glass is smashed but I still think they are his,' said Bert.

'What do you think, Richard?' Richard took the glasses and examined them closely. They look like Kevin's to me.'

'Yeah, definitely. So now we have broken glass and Kevin's glasses,' said Bert.

'Wow, it looks like blood here too.' The glasses had the same rusty looking blood stains on them as the broken glass.

'Come on, let's take both items to the police. They might help them find Kevin. If we are lucky, we might be able to speak to the detective who came to interview me.'

Richard pulled a handkerchief out and went and picked up the broken glass with the blood on it.

On the way to the police station, Bert pointed to a car on the side of the road. It was parked outside the grocery store. 'Isn't that the car we saw at the pub that night, the one you told the police about?'

Richard was sure it was – it had the same wood panels down the side. Just as Richard thought about checking out the licence plate, a woman came out of the grocer's shop yelling at a man in the car.

Mr Smith, the grocer, followed her out to the car, but the car took off. Richard didn't think quickly enough to get the numberplate. The woman looked very shaken and upset. Richard said they better remember to tell the police about this as well.

Chapter Four

Richard and Bert went to the police station, feeling pleased with what they had found, but on the other hand they were very anxious. Did this mean Kevin had been hurt? All they could do was take what they had to the police.

When they arrived, they went over to the desk. The desk sergeant was a bit overweight and going bald on top. He looked tall and imposing but had a friendly manner. 'Hello, lads,' he said, looking down at them. 'What can I do for you?'

Richard turned to Bert, who was looking away. 'Well, I suppose it's got to be me then, hasn't it.'

'You're the oldest, you do it,' Bert mumbled.

Richard was only weeks older than Bert, but Bert always used the excuse as a way out. Richard asked if they could see Detective Brown, that it was about Kevin Hughes.

'Okay, lads, wait here and I'll see if Detective Brown is available.'

Five minutes went by before Detective Brown appeared. 'Hello again, lads. What can I do for you, then? I hope you haven't been up to any mischief!'

Richard and Bert stepped back a bit, concerned.

Detective Brown saw the look on their faces and knew he must have frightened them. 'Sorry, lads. Didn't mean to scare you. Come on through and we will have a chat.'

The boys followed the detective through to his office and sat down.

'Right, what can I do for you?'

Richard looked at Bert, who still wasn't going to take the lead. 'We went to look for anything that might be related to Kevin's disappearance. We found these at Bonfire Hill.' He placed the glasses down gently onto the desk.

'What sort of rubbish is this?' Detective Brown asked.

The two boys did not expect this sort of reaction. 'No, you don't understand, we think these belong to Kevin,' said Richard.

The look on the detective's face changed. 'Oh, sorry, lads. Now I understand. Here let me have a good look at them.' Detective Brown also thought it looked like blood on the glasses but didn't say anything.

'We also found this,' said Bert, finally, handing over the broken glass.

Detective Brown nodded but didn't say anything. 'What about I drop you off at home and I will go and see Kevin's parents about the glasses, would that make you feel any better?'

'Oh, that's alright, we will walk home but thank you for offering.'

On the way out of the office, Bert remembered about the car and described it to Detective Brown. He asked if they had a registration number, and they felt embarrassed at not getting the chance to get it.

Detective Brown said, 'It's okay lads. This is a good thing that you have done. It could help us find Kevin, if it is confirmed the glasses are his, and it will all be down to you both and what you have found.' He put them into a plastic evidence bag and placed them in his pocket.

They both looked at each other and smiled feeling incredibly pleased at what had just been said. Once Richard and Bert left the station, they went straight to see Mr and Mrs Hughes. On the way, the excitement of their find wore off as they realised, they still didn't know where Kevin was or if he was okay. Moments after Detective Brown pulled up at the Hughes's, he saw Richard and Bert head towards the front door.

He knew it would be a difficult conversation if these were Kevin's glasses. As he stepped towards the house, there was such an eerie silence. The living room curtains were closed as it was appropriate as a mark of respect for the missing, or the death of a loved one.

'Looks like we're all here to see the Hughes's then,' he said. The boys jumped, not having seen him approach.

Mr Hughes opened the door. Richard looked up at Mr Hughes's huge frame, which made him look scary. He hadn't thought about how he would feel when he and Bert decided to come here. Richard could not help thinking about what Kevin had told him about his dad beating him and his mum. At this moment in time, there was nothing he could do about it; he had to try to not look as nervous as he was. Detective Brown being there made things a little bit better. They all went inside.

Mrs Hughes was sitting at the kitchen table with Owen; she had made sandwiches for their tea. She looked at all the people in the kitchen with a bit of shock, probably because she had not seen so many people together in her house since Kevin had gone. In a faint voice, a voice that sounded more like an old lady's voice, Mrs Hughes said hello to the boys and the detective. She looked very drawn and exhausted. Owen came over to Richard and Bert and gave them a big hug.

Detective Brown saw the opportunity to have a quiet word with the parents. 'Richard and Bert, why don't you take Owen and these sandwiches and go through to the lounge room while I speak to Mr and Mrs Hughes?'

Once the boys had gone, Detective Brown took out the items and put them on the table. Mrs Hughes gasped and raised a shaking hand to her mouth.

The glasses were Kevin's, they recognised them instantly. Seeing the blood-stained glass proved too much for Mrs Hughes. She began sobbing silently into a handkerchief.

Mr Hughes looked over to the detective. 'Where did you get them from?'

'Richard and Bert found them on Bonfire Hill. I brought them straight round here to see if you could identify them. Now that you have, this sheds a different light on the case.'

Mr Hughes looked shocked at what Detective Brown had just said. 'What do you mean by that? Are you trying to tell us Kevin is probably dead?'

'No, sir, please don't think that who can say what's on these glasses until we have them looked at. There could even be fingerprints or any kind of evidence. I am just saying that now we can get more officers on the case, and hopefully get some proof of where Kevin might be.'

This information didn't seem to settle Mr Hughes, but he nodded in agreement.

'Oh, there is something else, Mr Hughes. We have had a report of a minivan that we would like to speak to the owner about. Do you know anyone that drives a light blue Morris Minor with wood panels?'

Mr and Mrs Hughes shook their heads. They were glad the police now had some clues, but they were worried where they would now lead.

The boys were in the other room trying to console Owen. He talked about the good times they had shared watching Kevin playing footy with Richard and Bert.

Richard could not help feeling sad too. He knew Owen needed to be reassured. He bent down to Owen's level, and said, 'Owen, you must always remember that wherever he is, he loves you very much, and he always will. He used to tell me about all the funny things that you said and did to make him laugh when you were younger. Now you make sure that you always think about the happy times you had together. Will you do that for me Owen?'

With tears rolling down his face, he cuddled Richard. 'I will do. Will you come and see me more, and we can play football in the garden like I did with Kevin?'

Richard nodded. 'I will do. Maybe I could call to see you next weekend, would you like that?'

Owen smiled and wiped his eyes. 'Yes, I would. Will you come round for me?'

'We certainly will, won't we Bert.'

'Absolutely Owen, we will have to ask your parent's first though.'

Just then Detective Brown and Mr Hughes walked into the living room. Looking towards the boys, the detective told them he would see them again soon, then said goodbye.

Richard asked if he and Bert would be allowed to call round at weekends to play football with Owen on the field. Mr and Mrs Hughes were thrilled about their offer and immediately said yes.

'We'd better be going,' Richard said, not quite ready to stay there without the detective.

A knock at the front door drew the boys away. It was Owen's granny here to collect him to take him to the park to give his parent's a rest.

Mr Hughes saw them all to the front door and said goodbye to Richard and Bert and he was pleased to see Owen's grandmother as it meant that he and Brenda could talk in peace. Everyone left, leaving him and his wife together.

The house seemed so peaceful and quiet. Too quiet. They were not used to the silence. They both wished that their lives could be normal again, but deep down they both knew that was never going to happen. But for Brenda Hughes things were even worse, she still had the burden of knowing that her husband had something to do with the other woman that he had been seen with. There were days that she could hardly cope and all she wanted to do was cry all day long, but for Owen's sake she had to continue.

Both Brenda and Gavin had taken time off work, but time was going on and on with hardly any results. Gavin had to return to work the following week, or they would have other problems to deal with, like getting behind with their household bills.

Chapter Five

The detectives' next step was to interview the grocer that Richard and Bert had told him about, and to also talk to the upset lady who had talked to the man in the Morris Minor they were looking for. When the detectives arrived at the shop there were no customers which gave them the opportunity to speak to the shopkeeper while things were quiet.

Detective Brown introduced himself and his partner and said they had a few questions they would like to ask him.

'What can I do for you?' Mr Smith said, looking very confused as he had no idea what he could be of help with.

'We received information that one of your lady customers had a bit of an upset here the other day, and we were wondering if you could tell us about it.'

'Ah, yes, I remember. It was Mrs Betty Malone, from down the road. Two young men were leaving the store. Mrs Malone said one of them purposely pushed her out of temper and tried to knock her over on their way out. She was terribly upset about it.'

'Do you happen to know where she lives?'

'I pass her house every day and chat to her sometimes. If you stay on this side of the road, hers is the fourth house down, I think it has got pink curtains up at the windows.'

'Thank you, sir. You have been an immense help.'

The detectives left Mr Smith feeling immensely proud of himself for being able to help, even in such a small way.

As they approached the Malone residence, there were two ladies chatting outside the house. The ladies stopped talking and stared at the men as they walked towards them.

'Hello, ladies, sorry to interrupt. I'm Detective Brown and this is Detective Moore. We are wanting to speak with Betty Malone.'

The two women looked at each other.

'Yes, I'm Betty Malone,' one of the women said. 'What can I do for you?'

'Is it possible we could have a little chat with you inside?'

Mrs Malone said goodbye to her friend, then invited the detectives into her house. Her friend said goodbye, knowing that it would not be long before she found out what it was all about.

Mrs Malone asked them to take a seat in the lounge. 'Now, what is it you would like to talk to me about? I hope that lad of mine hasn't been up to anything.'

'We have information that a few days ago a young man physically assaulted you as you walked out of the grocer's shop up the road. Is this correct?'

'Well, yes, it is although I don't know if that is what you would call it. He did push into me hard, and on purpose, in fact so hard I nearly fell over, but I didn't report it. Who has been telling you all this? Was it someone from the shop?'

'No, not exactly. We are following up on information about the two men. Can you give us a description of them?'

'I think so.' Mrs Malone paused. 'Does this happen to have anything to do with the disappearance of that young lad, the poor little soul.'

'We are not sure if the matters are related,' said Detective Brown.

'Oh dear, that poor little boy, I hope you get all of this sorted out soon.'

'We intend to do our best, Mrs Malone.'

Pulling a cigarette out of her pack, she said, 'The bloke that pushed me was taller than the other one. He was probably about six foot tall. His mate was about five foot seven, or there about.'

'Thank you, that is extremely helpful. And the car they were driving. Did you notice anything about it?'

'Yes, I certainly did, just in case they were out to cause trouble elsewhere. I'm not too good at cars, but this one was a blue one, the kind with wood on the sides, it looked in good condition. And the smaller bloke was driving. To tell you the truth, the other one smelled of beer. I didn't get a licence plate number though.'

'I would like you to come into the station to give us a proper description of these two men. Would that be possible, Mrs Malone, then maybe we could get a photofit of them.'

After a little hesitation, Mrs Malone agreed. The detectives thanked her and left. Mrs Malone followed them out of the door, but instead of going back into her house she excitedly went to her friend's house to tell her the gossip.

The following morning, Mrs Malone was at the police station on the dot of ten o'clock. The sergeant was expecting her and took her through to Detective Brown's office. She had never done anything like this before and was a little bit nervous but felt more at ease when Detective Brown said he was pleased that she had turned up.

'Please, come in, Mrs Malone, take a seat.' He showed her over to a chair. A man was already seated opposite her. 'This is Jim Robbins, the sketch artist. He will ask you some questions.'

Mrs Malone lit a cigarette and started describing the tallest man first. He had quite a long thin face and a square jaw line, dark greased-back hair, you know in the style that the youngsters have it these days, clean shaven and I think his eyes were very dark brown.'

The artist started sketching as she went on to describe the shape of his mouth and nose.

'They looked a right pair of hooligans.'

Soon the sketch was finished, and the artist showed it to her.

'Oh, my goodness, that's exactly like him, but there's one thing you've missed off – the eagle tattoo on his neck.'

This comment could not have pleased Detective Brown more, as this was such a noticeable thing. Once the eagle was drawn onto the neck, Detective Brown looked at the sketch and smiled, then he showed it to Mrs Malone.

She excitedly said, 'Yep, that's definitely him.'

Detective Brown thought to himself, 'At last now we know who we are looking for.' He turned to Mrs Malone. 'You are doing well, Mrs Malone. Would you like a cup of tea?'

'A cup of tea will do nicely, thank you.'

The tea arrived within minutes, and she was soon ready to get onto the next description. She lit another cigarette. The next one was a little more difficult, at first.

'He was the smaller of the two and he didn't seem to be as tough looking like his mate. He had a roundish face, well, fat really, and he had a crew cut short to his head. I noticed that it made it look as though his ears stuck out. Oh, and I remember now! Once he got near the car, he shouted, "Come on Tom!" and that's when I noticed he had a broken top tooth, as though it was broken in half.'

Now the police had two photofit images that they could use. Detective Brown walked her to the door and thanked her for her help. He was thrilled with this latest information. Not only had he got a great outcome with the photofit images, but he also had a name. Straight away he started organising the pictures to be distributed to other police stations. The next stop was to see Mr and Mrs Hughes to see if they recognised these men.

When they arrived at the house that evening, it appeared dark and silent, and they did not expect anybody to be home, but Mr Hughes answered the door. He looked hopeful that they had finally brought them some good news.

Mrs Hughes was sitting in the living room and when they walked in, she looked at them and said nothing. She had begun to lose the small amount of faith she had in the police ever finding Kevin. Detective Brown felt a pang of sadness for her, he could see the poor lady was hurting badly. Mr Hughes, being a man, was holding it together as best he could.

'We've followed up on some leads and I have a few questions.' Detective Brown got out the photofit pictures to show them. 'Can you tell me if either of you have seen any of these two men before?'

They each took hold of one of the photofit pictures, but sadly neither of them recognised the men. Mrs Hughes looked up, tears rolling down her face. 'He's dead, isn't he? Why don't you stop giving us false hope and admit that you think he is dead, and we are never going to see our son again!'

Gavin held both of his wife's hands in his. 'Brenda. No, love, stop talking like that. We must hold on to every bit of hope we can find. We must have faith.'

Brenda quickly pulled her hands away from him. 'Faith! Faith in what, God?! If there was a God, he would not take our children away from us, would he.' She was sobbing so hard she could hardly get her breath.

Gavin held onto her tightly, there was nothing more that he could do.

Detective Brown, seeing the hurt and the upset they were both going through, said, 'I am so sorry, Mr Hughes, we are doing all we can, with extremely limited information to go on. But I promise you, we will be back as soon as we get any news for you.'

Gavin saw the detectives out, then sat and held Brenda's hand until she finally stopped crying, then he laid her on the couch with a cover over her, and she eventually fell asleep, sobbing silently, like an upset small child.

Weeks went by and still they had heard nothing more. Kevin had been missing for a couple of months now, and everybody suspected that he was never coming back, including Owen.

Richard had kept his promise to Owen and called round for him every weekend to play football, Owen had got so good at it, that he eventually played on the field with Kevin's other mates, and now they were a team again. Between this and his granny's love and support and the frequent stays at her house, it was good for Owen, as it kept his mind off everything else.

The detectives attempt to find the two men were not successful. In the beginning, the police were getting a lot of calls from the public saying that they had seen the two men, who were always together, or they had seen the car near shops or public houses, but by the time the police responded, they had gone.

The men were delaying detection, not staying in any place for longer than a couple of days. They must have known that the police were looking for them, they have probably seen their photofit pictures in newspapers, on walls at train stations, shops and other places, along with the description of their car.

Not long after the posters had gone up, the police received a report of a burnt-out vehicle in a field. The description matched the blue Morris Minor even down to the wood on the sides, with signs of light blue paint.

The field was sixty miles away, towards Blackpool.

The police got onto it straight away, and the car was indeed the one they had been looking for. This was not too good for the police, as it meant that the men had absconded further away from the area where Kevin had disappeared and could be just about anywhere. A forensic team checked the car, but unfortunately, they did not find any evidence.

It was now six months after Kevin's disappearance. The police approached Mr and Mrs Hughes about doing a television appeal in the hope Kevin had been sighted. Brenda refused. She was very unwell. Her nerves were so bad now, that she rarely left the house anymore. Brenda felt Kevin was never coming home. Someone, somewhere, knew something and all that was left now, was to be able to bring the culprits to justice, and hope they tell where Kevin's remains can be found.

As the one-year anniversary of Kevin's disappearance approached, Richard spoke to the head of the school to ask if a memorial service could be held during assembly. The principal agreed. It would be a whole school assembly in two days' time. On the day, the assembly hall looked immaculate, with flowers either side of the stage and a photograph of Kevin placed on a music stand on the centre of the stage. The pupils silently walked into the hall and took their seats.

The principal said that Kevin had been a remarkable student, always polite and helpful, and he would always be remembered by the school for the caring person that he was. Then the principal nodded to Richard who was seated on the stage ready to give the speech that he and his friends had written.

Richard began the speech; he kept calm and spoke so that everyone could hear his words. Halfway through, his voice began straining and the tears welled up in his eyes, but he managed to continue. The principal looked over to Richard to make sure he was all right to carry on but as he turned round, he could see that most of the young girls were crying silently, and the boys were really trying to keep it together, which for most of them was hard.

Richard and Bert could not wait for school to be over that day. They were feeling such strong emotions, ones they had never felt before, knowing that they now must accept that they will never see Kevin again. They planned to meet at Bonfire Hill after tea that evening to place some flowers for Kevin on the field, flowers Richard had asked his mum to get for him. When they arrived, the atmosphere was strained and quiet, each one of them having to contend with their own personal grief.

They sat down on the ground at the place where Richard had last seen Kevin. Richard placed the flowers down and sat quietly thinking. He went over and over the last conversation he had with Kevin, when Kevin told him about how he needs to protect his mum from his dad, and realising how sad Kevin was that he did not know how to help her.

There had been nothing Richard could do to help at the time. It had left him with a sense of 'if only' he had stayed and walked with him – 'if only' he hadn't had to go to the shop for his mum. Richard thought if all these things had been different, maybe Kevin could still be here, and his parents would not be suffering day after day, waiting for Kevin to be found.

The boys sat for a while chatting about the good times that they had shared. The fun times, where they had made each other laugh by doing things like seeing who could pull the most stupid face and who could fart the loudest. Such childish things but they were the things that brought them together as loyal friends. After a while, they walked around the area, remembering more good times they shared with Kevin, especially on bonfire nights.

After they had walked a bit further and were headed home, Bert said, 'I forgot to tell you.'

Richard turned to Bert with a look of dread on his face. Whenever Bert said those first few words, it normally meant that he had forgot something important.

'My mum was talking to someone the other day, and she said that she had heard that the police had found the car they'd been looking for in Blackpool, but nothing became of it.'

This comment made Richard feel so low. Now they will always be wondering where their friend is. Kevin might never be found, but he will always be the friend that they will never forget.

Chapter Six

Two years had now gone by, and Richard had left school. He now worked as an apprentice joiner and was doing very well. There was not a day that went by that he did not think about Kevin, every day hoping that he might come home.

Richard and a couple of other friends would meet at Bonfire Hill now and again, just to sit and talk about their missing friend, in some way hoping that he could hear them and know that he will never be forgotten.

It was quite different for Gavin and Brenda; they would never come to terms with the loss of their beautiful boy. He was a missing part of them. Brenda found it hard to cope with everyday life, while Gavin stayed strong enough to continue. He knew that every day that went by, his wife's heart broke that little bit more, so much so, she would never return to work again.

Gavin also weathered the glares from some of the neighbours when they saw him in the street; their looks were obviously saying they thought he was guilty of doing something to Kevin himself, remembering the time they saw him taken away in the detective's car and jumping to their own conclusions. These were all heavy burdens on top of the loss of his son.

Brenda's mother had passed away during the last year,

something that tore another hole in their already broken hearts. Owen's Granny had been like a second mum to him, and he missed her as much as he missed Kevin.

Owen was soon going to be thirteen years old, and he tried to help his mum get through each day as best he could. For a child of his age, it was such a heavy burden to carry, but he made sure that he spent as much time with her as possible. He was doing well at school and becoming a kind and considerate person, always wanting to help in any way that he could. His favourite subject was sport. Owen and his dad had become remarkably close, both knowing that they had to do all they could to help his mum to get herself back to the person she once was. That was never going to happen, as she still had the added heartache of knowing about the woman that her husband had been meeting at the canal, she could not let it go. It was tearing her apart.

Brenda's condition gradually deteriorated. Alone in the house after seeing Owen off to school, she would walk around talking to herself, asking and answering her own questions – mainly about the other woman. Perhaps this was a way she avoided thinking about Kevin. Things were getting very bad with her mental state, and she decided to walk to the canal, which is about a twenty-minute walk, in the hope that the other 'woman' might be there. Even though she had no idea what 'that woman' looked like, she couldn't stop thinking about it, she was telling herself aloud, 'That's what I'll do, I'll walk along the canal looking for her, and I'll find out why she was talking to my husband in secret.'

She had been to the canal many times slowly walking and talking to herself. People would walk by and look at her as if to say, 'You need your head looking at, lady.'

none of them knowing what she had been through. People are so quick to form their own opinions sometimes. Brenda was grieving deeply. She knew she was expected to 'get on with it,' but she couldn't.

Brenda sometimes sat down on the grass to rest for a while, to watch the people passing her by. Some walked their dogs, some even said hello to her, and she would say hello back, while others, who were frequent visitors, would ignore her as they now saw her as someone not quite right in the head. Her visits would only last about an hour or so, then she would wander back home again.

She told Gavin about her walks along the canal, thinking that he would tell her not to go there recalling that's where he had met the other woman, but he didn't say anything like that, he just said he thought it was a good idea, and the fresh air would do her good. But she didn't ever tell him the real reason she went there. Once the warm weather disappeared and the wintry weather had started to come in, her visits to the canal became less frequent.

On this day, Brenda was not feeling her best. Her depression didn't seem to be getting any better, and her medication had been increased which caused violent headaches and dizziness, which she had been told were all part of the side effects and would soon stop once she had got used to the new dose.

She put on her coat and boots, and off she went to the canal. When she arrived, she was surprisingly the only person there. Perhaps people must think it is too cold to be out walking, but at least it was peaceful.

She walked along the canal path, closer and closer to the edge, thinking, 'I could easily end it all. I could jump into the water and drown myself. Once I'm in there, I wouldn't be able to get out because I can't swim. Then I could be with Kevin again.' She looked up to the sky, hoping Kevin would be looking down on her. She almost did fall in when she was startled by a dog barking behind her. As she turned, it came running towards her. It was a beautiful black Labrador.

'Lucy, Lucy, come here,' a woman shouted after the dog.

As the woman put the lead on Lucy, Brenda told her what a lovely dog she had and tried to start up a conversation with her, but the woman didn't seem to want to bother with her.

Brenda, having not seen her before, asked, 'Do you live far from here?'

'No, just a few streets away, after the next bridge.'

'Oh, what's your name, I will watch out for you next time.'

'Cathy. Sorry, can't stop. I must get on.'

Then before she knew it the woman disappeared under the canal bridge and was gone. Brenda began to walk slowly back home, enjoying the fresh air when suddenly she realised something. The woman she had exchanged a few words with at the canal had a Welsh accent, like Gavin. But she didn't take in the importance of it as her mind wasn't in the right place at the time.

When she arrived home, the house was nice and quiet, so she ran herself a bath. She lay in the bath for what seemed like ages, soaking up the warmth and quiet. Then the sudden realisation of what had happened hit her.

'Oh my God, what have I done? Oh no! I was thinking

about committing suicide. What is wrong with me?' She got out of the bath, crying hysterically.

She heard the back door slam open, just like Kevin used to do, and Owen shouted out, 'I'm home, Mum. Where are you?'

Brenda panicked at hearing Owen's voice but tried to sound as calm as possible. 'Oh, hello love, I've just finished having a bath, I'll be down in a few minutes.'

'Okay, Mum. Would you like me to make you a cup of tea?'

'That would be lovely, Owen, thank you.' With every word Brenda spoke she knew the panic was still in her voice and Owen might notice it. A few minutes later she was dressed and downstairs to see Owen, trying to stay as calm as she could. They sat at the dining table to have their tea.

Owen could sense something was not right. 'Are you alright Mum? You look as though you have been crying.'

Trying to sound calm, Brenda said, 'Yes, I'm fine, Kevin!'

They looked at each other in shock and horror.

'Oh, oh, my goodness, I'm so sorry, Owen. I didn't mean to say that. It just slipped out.' She stood up and went to cuddle him. 'I don't know what's wrong with me lately.' Brenda burst into tears.

'Mum, it's okay. Kevin was my brother it's obvious that he is still on your mind. I knew there was something wrong. Tell me what it is.'

Brenda took a deep breath. 'I went for a walk to the canal today for a bit of fresh air, but I really don't know what happened, Owen, truly I don't.'

'Mum, what is it? What have you done?'

'It doesn't matter, Owen. I'm okay now. I'm not really coping very well. I have days when things get too much for me, and as you heard, I called you Kevin.' She took hold of Owen's hand. 'I think I thought about killing myself while I was at the canal, and that's something I will never do. I love you and your dad so much, although he can have a bad temper sometimes. I can't stand to think that my beautiful son is out there somewhere all alone. We need to find him. I will not settle until we do. My heart is broken, I think it is never going to mend.' With the realisation of what had happened, Brenda knew she needed professional help.

'Come on, Mum, come and sit down in the living room. I will get you a blanket, so you can have a rest.'

'Alright, Owen, but don't let me fall asleep. I need to start preparing dinner for when your dad gets home from work.'

Owen sat with his mum knowing that she had been so upset from the ordeal that she had been through, and would soon fall asleep, which is what he wanted. In ten minutes, Brenda was fast asleep. Owen went out to see Richard. He could talk to Richard about anything, and Richard would be able to tell him what to do. When Owen arrived at Richard's house, Richard's mum answered the door.

'Hello, love, what's brought you here in the freezing cold? How's your mum doing?'

'She's not too good at the moment, Mrs Marshall,' Owen said, looking down at the floor, hoping that she wouldn't notice his sadness.

'Oh dear, please send her my love. Come on in, Richard's upstairs in his bedroom as usual. I think he would like to live up there. Just go on up to him if you want.'

Owen walked into Richard's room, and he was sitting reading a comic.

Richard looked shocked to see him. 'Hello Owen, what's wrong, mate, are you okay?'

Owen was relieved to be with Richard and hoped that he could help him in some way. Owen told Richard everything about his mum thinking about committing suicide and calling him Kevin.

'What do you think I should do, Richard? I don't want my mum to die.'

'I know you don't, Owen. Everything will be alright in the end. I think the only thing you can do is to tell your dad, but don't mention the suicide thing because your mum asked you not too, just tell him that you came home and found her sobbing.'

'Yeah, but she does that anyway.'

'I know, but this time it was different. Tell him that she thought you were Kevin, and that she needs to see the doctor again.'

Owen was grateful to have a friend like Richard. He could always go to him with any worries he might have.

A few days later Gavin took Brenda to the doctors and her medication was changed. Thankfully the new medication worked, and Brenda slowly but surely began to calm down. But the thought of this other woman was still on her mind, and she knew she had to get to the bottom of it, but she didn't know where to begin.

Chapter Seven

A couple of weeks later Owen was walking back home after spending the afternoon at his mate's house, when Richard came shouting after him. 'Wait there, Owen! I've got something to tell you.' By the time Richard caught up to Owen, he was out of breath.

'It's okay Rich, slow down. What's the matter? It must be something important.'

'Yes, it is. You're not going to believe it.' Richard got his breath back and they carried on walking. 'My mum told me that one of the blokes from the photofit pictures has been arrested. She heard it on the radio. He has been taken to the police station for questioning.'

In Owen's young mind, all he could envision was this man being put in prison and his Mum getting better because he had been caught. 'What! I'd better get home to let Mum and Dad know,' Owen said.

'I'll let you know what happens tomorrow, maybe the police have rung my mum and told her. I'd better get home to her quick.'

Owen ran the rest of the way home without stopping. He barged through the back door, in the same way his brother used to do, shouting, 'Mum, Dad, where are you?'

'Oh, my goodness, Owen, what on earth is the matter? Did you have to charge through the door like that? It nearly came off its hinges.'

Owen's dad also heard the commotion and went to see what it was all about.

Owen blurted out what Richard had told him, but his parents hadn't had any phone call from the police. Gavin put his coat on straight away to go round to the police station.

Brenda turned to her husband. 'Oh my God, what could this mean? Gavin, do you think he was the one who took Kevin away from us?'

'I don't really know, Brenda. Listen, love, don't get yourself too excited. We don't even know which one has been arrested, but either way it's good news. Let's slow down a little first.'

'But Gavin, it doesn't really matter which one it is. What we do know is that they were more than likely both involved in taking Kevin away from us.' Brenda could not believe how calm Gavin was being and went to get her coat. 'We need to get round there now. Come on, love, we will go together.'

Owen put his arms around his mother's waist and calmly said, 'Mum, it's okay I will stay here with you while Dad goes.'

Gavin had to approach what he was going to say next, very carefully. He had to be sensitive towards Brenda's feelings. 'Brenda, listen to me, love. If you come with me, you will only start getting yourself upset and I won't be able to ask the questions that I need to ask, that's if I even get to see Detective Brown. Please, love, wait here. Owen will stay with you.'

Brenda reluctantly gave in and let her husband go on his own. As soon as he had gone, she went to look at the newspaper clippings she'd taken of the photofits. She found herself staring at them thinking to herself that they must be the people who took Kevin. But where had they taken him, and what had they done to him?

Gavin walked to the police station in the hope that he could clear his mind, all the while thinking to himself what questions he would ask Detective Brown and what the next stage would be. He arrived at the police station, still not sure of what he was going to say.

Two other people were at the counter. A lady at the desk with her back to him, and a man inside sitting down. He went back outside and smoked a cigarette, hoping that the other two people would be gone soon. When he walked back in, the woman was still talking to the desk sergeant, but the man had left. Gavin sat down to wait.

'Right, Mrs Patterson, the information that I have is that the person you are enquiring about will not be allowed out today, he has to face court in the morning.'

'Okay, that's fine. At least I know. And it's not Mrs Patterson, it's Miss Davis.'

'Oh, sorry, love, my mistake. I thought you had said you were his mum.'

'No, he's a friend of my son. They work together.'

The woman's voice sounded familiar, then when she walked away from the desk, Gavin followed her. The last time he had seen this woman was at the canal.

'Oh my God, it's you! Catherine Davis! Why are you here, at this police station on the same day as I am? This is some coincidence.'

Catherine glared at him, and said, with hate in her voice, 'Think about this. I could ask you the very same question, couldn't I?' She began to walk away.

Gavin grabbed her arm. 'Don't you dare walk away from me. Don't you think that I deserve an apology from you for making my life a misery, nearly ruining my marriage?'

'Get your hands off me or I will go back inside the station and get you arrested for assault. Now take your hands off me and leave me alone.'

This woman had tried to destroy him, and he wanted to know why. Gavin let go of her arm and blocked her way, demanding answers.

She was so angry. 'Okay, you asked for it. I'll tell you why I left Wales and came here. I had been looking for you for years, then three years ago, I found out where you lived and work, so we left Wales and came here to get what you owe me. Believe me, you're not going to think yourself so wonderful when I've finished with you.'

Gavin wondered what she was talking about, and what he had done to make her hate him so much. 'What the hell are you talking about, woman, and who's 'we'.

'Do you remember all those years ago back home in Wales, before you decided to finish with me, so that you could come and live here in England with your nice new girlfriend? And if I remember correctly, isn't her name Brenda?' she said all of this in a sarcastic manner, and then put her face right up to his. 'Well, I was pregnant with your son, not that you cared.'

'What! Oh, don't come that with me. I'm sick to death of you and your lies. I've heard it all before, one minute you were pregnant then the next you weren't. You ought to try making your mind up.' Gavin didn't know what to believe. 'If all that is true, why the hell didn't you tell me in the beginning? Why have you left it all these years? You could have told me when we met up at the canal, but you chose not to, so what the hell was all that about? Did you want to make me suffer a bit longer, having to put up with all your nasty little threats?'

'No, I wanted you and your wife to suffer. It's taken me years to find out where you lived. In fact, when I saw you both at the canal that time, the look on your face said it all. The woman I had been chatting to, was your wife, wasn't she. And that's what I have come for, to enjoy destroying you and your wife, just like you destroyed my life, leaving me alone penniless, trying to bring up YOUR child. You owe me big time.' She turned to walk away.

There was no way that he was going to leave everything unfinished. Gavin grabbed her arm again. 'Oh no you don't. Now you have finally decided to tell me that I have got a son that I never knew about, now you can tell me the rest. It's been twenty years or more, for God's sake.'

'What do you mean, the rest? Like what?' Catherine's hatred was clear.

Gavin decided he was getting nowhere with her, so he tried to change the conversation. He wondered if her visit here had anything to do with her son. 'Catherine, tell my why you were in the police station? Has your son been hurt or something? And speaking of 'our' son, you could at least have the decency to tell me his name.'

Catherine looked at Gavin and with a huge smile on her face said, 'His name is Thomas, Thomas Hughes to be exact, and you owe me twenty years maintenance for him. Oh, look, my bus is coming,' she said, then she sarcastically added, 'so goodbye,' and shaking off his arm, stepped onto the bus.

Gavin knew that there was nothing more he could do, but he couldn't help thinking that Catherine was in such a bad temper, and every word was said with hatred in her voice that she must be telling the truth about her having his son. Feeling confused and angry he returned to the police station. Once inside, he asked the desk sergeant if he could speak to Detective Brown. Gavin waited quietly, all of what had happened going round and round in his mind, not only about the child he never got to know, but about the reason he was here waiting to see Detective Brown. Thank God Brenda had stayed home.

'Ahh, hello, Mr Hughes. I was just about to call you. I have some news for you. Come through to my office.'

Detective Brown could see Gavin was in a bit of a state and offered him a drink of water, which he gratefully accepted. 'Firstly, what can I do for you, Mr Hughes? I suppose you have heard about the arrest of one of the lads from the photofit?'

'Is it true? Is it one of them?'

'Yes, I'm pleased to say that it is.'

'Does this mean that we are getting closer to finding out what happened to Kevin? Can you show me which one it is that has been arrested?'

Detective Brown picked up the photofit and showed it to Gavin. 'We now have a full name for him. His name is Simon Patterson. He was arrested for burglary.'

'Burglary? I thought you would be telling me there was evidence of him being involved with my son's disappearance.'

'Not yet, Mr Hughes. We haven't interviewed him fully yet. He has a long list of offences to his name so I think he will soon be spending time at Her Majesty's Pleasure.'

'So, what you're telling me is that he hasn't actually been arrested over the disappearance of my son?' Gavin was confused. 'Detective Brown, you have told me that you have this lad in custody, and you have his full name, Simon Patterson—'

As soon as Gavin said the name, he recalled the desk sergeant calling Catherine Mrs Patterson when she was stood at the front desk. Everything was getting on top of him, his mind was racing, and he could no longer think straight. He made excuses that he had to leave and thanked Detective Brown. He walked home slowly, thinking to himself what a waste of time that visit was.

He knew that he had to tell Brenda the upsetting news that Simon Patterson was arrested for burglary rather than for the disappearance of their son. He also knew how this news would upset her and start off her depression again. He sat down on the park bench and smoked a couple of cigarettes, thinking about the other devastating news that Catherine had told him, about the child he never knew he had.

He remembered what Catherine had told the sergeant, that she wasn't Simon Patterson's mother. This meant the other one the police were looking for could be his son. What would he tell Brenda? He knew the right thing to do was to tell her, but in the end, he decided not to, for everybody's sake.

When he arrived home, Brenda and Owen rushed to the door excitedly wanting to hear the news. They were shocked to hear that Simon Patterson had not been arrested for Kevin's disappearance.

'I am so sorry that I can't give you the news that we all wanted to hear. I'm as upset as you two are, but now you know why I thought it was best for you not to come with me.'

Brenda looked at Gavin with tears falling from her eyes. Then sobbing, she said to him, 'I thought that they were going to tell us that he had admitted he was involved in Kevin's disappearance. Then maybe, we could finally find and bury our son. But now none of that is going to happen. How many more years have we got to put up with this torture? All I want is to bring home my beautiful boy.'

'I know you do, love. That's all any of us want. Hopefully Detective Brown will be able to get a confession out of him soon, or at least some kind of information that can be followed up. We will have to wait and see.'

Wiping the tears away from her eyes, Brenda said, 'When did he say he will be in contact with us again?'

'The lad is in court tomorrow so we will have to wait and see how things go. For now, all we can do is hope.'

Gavin and Brenda did not attend the hearing. Afterwards, detectives informed them that Simon Patterson was looking at five years, at least, for multiple misdemeanours, but they had nothing on him for Kevin's disappearance.

Months went by, and while Simon was in prison, he had a visitor, who he expected to be Tom, but he was wrong. The person was not anyone he knew. He walked over to his allocated table, not knowing what was going on, all the time looking at the person in front of him, thinking, 'I can't place who this person is. I don't think I have ever met him before.'

Simon sat down slowly and asked him his name.

The man totally ignored his question. 'I've been sent here by Tom.'

Straight away Simon knew he was here to deliver a warning. He could tell by the tone of his voice.

'Tom said to tell you that if you breath one word about that kid or the other business, you are dead. Don't forget there are a few people in here that will be watching you. If you go opening your mouth about the drug deals or the kid to anybody, the next time you go to the showers you will not be coming out alive. Got it?'

Simon knew his life was at stake, but he just couldn't cope with the worry of knowing that people were out to kill him. He couldn't take any more of it, and decided to go to see the prison warden and told him everything about the robberies, the drugs, and the murder of Kevin Hughes, including the name of his accomplice, Tom Hughes. He was put into solitary confinement for protection until everything he had told them was checked. None of this would help him. Simon hung himself in his cell that night.

The information from Simon was passed straight on to the police so they could deal with it, and they could apprehend Thomas Hughes. The police realised that through his prison connections, Hughes would have heard about Simon committing suicide. They knew they would have their work cut out trying to find him and began a search.

Weeks had gone by and eventually he was apprehended while hiding in his mother's loft. She didn't know anything about what he had done and was shocked when she saw her son being dragged down the stairs and into a police vehicle. She said they had the wrong man.

He was sentenced to twenty-five years in prison. The police had informed Gavin and Brenda about the development, and when they told them his name, Gavin looked at the police officer, shocked. Tom, the son that he didn't know he had, had killed his other son, Kevin.

Brenda and Owen tried their best to console Owen, but it would be a long time before any of them came to terms with what had happened. They hoped the police would find Kevin soon, so that he could be put to rest.

Chapter Eight

With no further news from the police, Gavin and Brenda had finally come to terms that they may never know what has happened to Kevin. It had now been nearly three years. At least Brenda was more of herself these days. Gavin had started accompanying Brenda on some of her canal walks, just to be together for a short time and for Gavin to try to show Brenda how sorry he was for what he had done.

They were both enjoying the sunshine, when they met a friend of Gavin's and stopped to chat to him. Brenda noticed a familiar face and said to Gavin, 'I'm just going over to talk to somebody that I know, Gavin. I won't be long.' She walked off before Gavin could ask her who it was.

Gavin was still busy chatting and did not really take much notice of what Brenda had said but, halfway through a conversation, he glanced over to where Brenda was, and instantly stopped talking. He could not believe his eyes. Brenda was talking to Catherine Davis. Gavin thought he was dreaming, thinking, 'No! this cannot be happening. What the hell is going on?' Gavin was so distraught by this that he became oblivious to anything his mate was saying.

'Gav, Gav, what's the matter with you?' his friend said. 'Are you okay, mate? You look as though you've seen a ghost.'

Gavin tried to look and sound normal. 'Oh sorry, I was completely out of it then. I don't know what happened. I'm okay now, thanks, mate. I better get back to Brenda.'

To Gavin's relief, by the time he'd turned back, Brenda was already walking back to him. Gavin and Catherine glared at each other, then she turned and walked away in the opposite direction. Gavin tried to stay as calm as possible and asked Brenda who the woman was, trying to make it look as though he had never seen her before.

'Oh, it's just somebody that I met here ages ago, I've only seen her that one time when she was walking her dog here. Her name is Cathy.'

Gavin could not believe his luck when he realised that Brenda had not put two and two together and realised that this woman is Catherine. Catherine must not have mentioned anything to Brenda about the child.

Deep down he knew Catherine was nasty enough to keep that little snippet of information to herself until the day that she needed it. On the walk home Brenda noticed that Gavin was extremely quiet, she began wondering what could have made him like that as he was fine before she had gone talking to Cathy. Gavin hardly said a word to her which made Brenda start to think she had done or said something wrong.

Weeks passed after the canal incident, with Gavin dreading every day, thinking Catherine could have found out where he lived and might call in unexpected at any time. He was by this time under so much stress, he didn't know how much more he could take. The thought of her doing that made him make the decision to tell Brenda knowing it will break her heart, but he knew it had to be done.

For the next few weeks, he tried hard to pick up the courage to tell her, but he just couldn't do it.

The weeks went by, and Gavin's moods and guilt were getting too much for him to bear, and he decided to tell Brenda who the woman at the canal was. He waited till the weekend came round for the two of them to be in the house alone once Owen had gone out with his mates to play football.

Then he saw the chance to approach Brenda. He sat her down facing him. He held her hands, which made Brenda straight away think to herself that something was drastically wrong, but she knew she had to hear him out.

The part about Catherine having a child to him, and she had given the child their name was too much for her to bear, and she knew from that moment on her life would never be the same again. She couldn't come to terms with the fact that Gavin's other son had killed Kevin.

She couldn't stand the thought of Gavin being near her, so she told him that from now on he will be sleeping in the living room, and not to say a word about the child, to anybody, especially Owen. This went on for months, and there was no sign of their marriage ever returning to normal.

One evening Brenda was in the kitchen dishing up the evening meal and Gavin was in the living room watching television. When she shouted for Gavin to come in to cut the meat for dinner, he did not answer. She thought that he must have the television so loud he couldn't hear her, so she went into tell him.

Gavin looked as though he was asleep, so Brenda shook him, but he didn't move. She shook him again a little bit harder, but still no response.

By this time, it was obvious to her that something was drastically wrong. The way Gavin's head lolled to one side, she thought he must be dead. Gavin looked as though he had fallen asleep and died peacefully. Brenda screamed Owen's name, and he came running out of the bedroom.

'What's wrong, Mum, are you alright?'

'Owen, come downstairs quickly. I think there is something wrong with your dad. Help me with him, he's on the couch and I can't turn him round.'

Owen ran down the stairs, and he threw open the living room door. His dad, still and not breathing, was a sight that hit him straight away. Brenda attempted to call for an ambulance but was unable to speak clearly enough on the phone, so Owen took the phone from her and told them what had happened. The receptionist told him an ambulance would be there immediately.

Owen then went to take care of his mum. She was walking around in shock and disbelief, crying like an injured dog. The sound from his mum is something that he will never forget. This is something a twelve-year-old child would find extremely hard to cope with and the memory of it will stay with him for many years to come.

Chapter Nine

The ambulance arrived in ten minutes, and they confirmed the death. Brenda screamed as Gavin was taken away from her for the very last time. She was sure it must have been the extent of the stress the other woman had put on him by hounding him and then telling him about the child that had killed him.

She grabbed at the man's arm trying to stop him taking her love away from her. Her sobbing, and the look on her face will be something Owen would never forget. Brenda was so distraught with grief she found it hard to breath. The ambulance officer gave her something to help calm her nerves. As they were leaving, they asked Owen if there was anyone who could come round to be with him, so the neighbour was asked to sit with them both.

After a couple of hours, Brenda calmed down a little, or perhaps she had gone into shock. Brenda thanked the neighbour for being with them but told her she now needed to go to bed as the medication had begun to take effect. Owen helped his mum up the stairs and when Brenda was in bed, she threw her arms around Owen and held him tight, thinking to herself how brave he was to be able to have done what he did and having called for help, staying calm at such a dreadful time.

Leaving his Mum alone to rest, Owen then went back downstairs and phoned Richard, telling him what had happened. He asked him to come round to stay with him for a while. Owen was trying to speak clearly in between sobbing. Richard stayed until late that evening and made sure they were both all right before he left. Brenda was still sleeping.

Richard had been like a brother to Owen since Kevin had disappeared. There were no longer many relatives nearby, and most of the friends they did have had not spoken to Brenda and Gavin since Kevin's disappearance, all of them blaming Gavin.

Gavin was buried ten days later in the local cemetery. Brenda never recovered from the loss of her husband and son. She began to rely increasingly on Owen to take care of most things.

A few days after the funeral, Detective Brown called round. Owen answered the door.

'Hello Owen, nice to see you again. Would it be okay to speak to your dad, please, that's if he's in?'

Sadness crossed Owen's face. Owen invited the detective in and directed him to Brenda who was sitting in the living room, not doing anything but staring into space.

Detective Brown was shocked when he saw Brenda. She didn't so much as turn her head to see who was coming through the door. He knew something was terribly wrong. 'Is there something wrong, Owen? Where's your dad?'

Owen moved closer to him so that his mum could not hear what they were saying. She was so fragile and broken. With tears in his eyes, he said, 'My dad passed away a couple of weeks ago. He died of a heart attack and his funeral was a few days ago. As you can see, my mum isn't doing too good. I'm very worried about her. She isn't sleeping and hardly eats anything. I don't know what to do.'

Gavin had always looked extremely healthy, a little bit overweight but that was all. News of his death was a shock to Detective Brown. 'I'm so sorry to hear that Owen, I can see that your mum isn't doing so good. Is there anything we can do for you?'

'Well, apart from finding my brother and bringing my dad back, there's not much you can do. Friends and neighbours call in to make sure we are alright, and Richard calls round whenever he can. I'm hoping he can help me to get mum to talk to us, and maybe eat something.'

'I hope you don't mind me suggesting this, Owen, but I think it would be a good idea to get the doctor round to see your mum. She might need some medical help.' Detective Brown said.

'Yes, she has been given the proper medication and the chemist delivers the prescription for her when she needs it.'

'Oh, that's good. Could you give her a message for me? Just tell her I will ring her tomorrow, as it's important that I speak to her.' The message that Detective Brown needed to relay to Brenda, was that Simon Patterson had committed suicide, but he didn't want to tell her in front of Owen.

The next day the doctor arrived to check on Brenda's health. He took one look at her and knew she was in a bad way. He prescribed her some different medication.

As the weeks went by, Brenda was getting a little bit stronger every day, but it took her a lot longer to get used to Gavin not being there with her. She sometimes thought that she could sense his presence and smell his aftershave, but she would always put it down to her imagination. Then the memory of what Gavin had told her would come flooding back, and yet she could not forgive him.

Richard visited them often, mainly at weekends after his long working week, to check on Brenda and to play football with Owen in the back garden, hoping this would help keep things as normal as possible for him.

After a few more months, the two women that his mum used to work with dropped by the house. These were the same women that had spread the rumours that Gavin had something to do with Kevin's disappearance because they had seen him getting into the police car. They had stopped speaking to the family years ago and had never done anything to help when Gavin died.

Yet here they were at the front door.

'Hello, Owen.' The ladies looked uncomfortable. 'I hope you don't mind us calling round, but if it's okay we would like to speak to your mum please.'

'What are your names? I will tell her you are here.'

'I'm Gladys and this is Irene.'

'Alright wait there and I will tell her, she hasn't been very well.'

Owen thought, 'Of all the cheek. They haven't spoken to my mum and dad for years, and they turn up wanting to speak to her now.'

Before he knew it, he could not stop himself saying what he had just thought.

The two women looked at each other. 'Yes, we know, Owen. We are sorry. We have come round now to apologise to you both. What we did was nasty and selfish, and we can't tell you how sorry we are for how we have treated you all.'

'Right. Okay then, but you better not start upsetting my mum. She's been through enough over the years.' Owen showed them into the living room. Brenda was sitting alone, staring at the television. 'Mum, there's people here to see you.'

Brenda looked up to see them but then turned away.

Gladys moved closer to her. 'Hello, Brenda, it's Gladys and I have got Irene with me, how are you?' She held Brenda's hand. 'I know we haven't bothered with any of you for years, but we are here now to tell you how sorry we are for treating you the way we did, and especially for ignoring you when we saw you in the street. We can't tell you how sorry we are to hear about Gavin, we hope you can accept our apology.'

Brenda turned and said, 'Now why should I do that?'

These were the most words his mum had spoken in a long time. Owen was shocked but pleased. The women sat either side of Brenda while Owen made them all a cup of tea. They sat chatting to her for a while, and Brenda did her best to speak back to them.

As time went on, the atmosphere became more relaxed, until in the end they were having a conversation about when they all worked at the factory together and recalling the names of some of the people that they worked with.

By the time they had finished talking, Brenda seemed like a new person. Owen realised that all she needed was friends by her side again, to help her heal from the torment that she has suffered for years. The two women left about forty minutes later, saying that they will be back to see her in a couple of days.

Brenda continued getting better and stronger by the day. She had started to go out again and meet up with her friends, although it was a long time before she could begin to heal fully. She was still broken by the loss of her son and husband, and she found the whole situation about Tom Hughes very hard to cope with, but she kept that information to herself.

The police seemed to be doing nothing to help find Kevin. Everything was at a standstill. It was almost as if Kevin's disappearance had been forgotten.

Brenda was getting herself ready to go out one day and meet up with her friends when there was a knock on the door. She answered it and it was Catherine Davis. Brenda was shocked to see her and could not believe the cheek of the woman who wanted to break up her family.

'What on earth are you doing here?' Brenda said. 'I would like you to leave right now.'

'Would you now? Not before I see that husband of yours. I want the payment that he owes me.'

'Payment for what? Don't tell me you think he is going to pay for the child you had, or say you had to him,' said Brenda.

'Oh, so he had the guts to tell you about it then, did he?'

'Yes, he did. You had stressed him to the limit. I don't

think he could take any more from you, and you killed him in the end. He had a heart attack. And your son killed my Kevin.'

Catherine didn't know what to say, and just stood and looked at Brenda, then quietly turned around and walked away.

A week later a hand-delivered letter arrived, addressed to Brenda and Owen. Somehow Catherine had found out that Gavin had another son named Owen.

Owen picked up the letter and took it to his mum who was in the kitchen. Because it had his name written on, he opened it. He took out the letter thinking it was going to be something nice from someone he knew but he couldn't believe what he was reading.

> *Dear Brenda and Owen,*
>
> *Please forgive me for the upset I have caused your family. I didn't know about Gavin's death until you told me. I just needed him to pay towards the years I struggled trying to bring up his son. I do not believe my son Tom had anything to do with the death of your boy. I am sorry for your loss, and I am so sorry for the way I behaved when I saw you. I wish you and your son no harm,*
>
> *Catherine.*

'Mum, this letter has just been posted through the door.' Owen looked as if he was about to burst into tears. 'What does it mean?'

Brenda saw the look on Owen's face and knew that it was something he really shouldn't have opened. She read the letter, there was nothing she could do but tell the truth to Owen about his half-brother.

Brenda took hold of Owen and held him tightly in her arms as if she would never let go, but deep down in some way she was glad all the lies were now out in the open and they could get on with their lives together as best they could, without the two people that should have still been there with them.

Chapter Ten

The year was 1994. Serena Jackson, a psychic medium, was suddenly woken from a deep sleep. She was receiving a message from a murder victim whose body had never been found.

Serena was often contacted through the spirit world, by the spirit of the deceased, in the hope that she would be able to help find their remains and then they could be laid to rest in consecrated ground, and the families will finally have closure.

When Serena received a message, she would write the information down as quickly as possible to make sure that she does not leave anything out. She needs all the information she can get. She is often told a lot of information in a brief period. These victims need her help and so do their families, and she will do all she can to help get their loved one's remains found, no matter how tough this is going to be, it must be done.

Serena went downstairs taking her notes with her, had breakfast, then spent the day investigating what she was shown in her vision. When working on a case, she always had her most important piece of paper with her, the one that she wrote as soon as she could after receiving the message. In this message she had been given quite a lot of information. She read over it again.

Wooded area with buttercups, rocks that Kevin the victim, called large flat rocks and, three huge, tall black rocks a way in the distance. The tall black ones are the ones where his remains could be found, although Kevin hadn't mentioned a name for the rocks. At least she had been given some details about the culprits. She couldn't help thinking that this was going to be a very difficult case as she didn't know anything about the area, or the danger she would be putting herself and her sister in if they investigated.

From experience, Serena knew that going to the police with any of this information would be a complete waste of time, as they do not listen to any psychic information at all. Still, Serena understood this was her life's purpose. This is what she was put on this earth to do.

Often when a spirit message comes through, Serena can see everything else as though it is a film playing out in front of her eyes, and during this experience everything feels so distant. In the spirit world, there is no time or distance continuum, which is why mediums from one country can speak to a spirit from another country. She felt the pain and the emotion of the poor innocent victim, experiencing how their death happened.

The child she had received information about should have had his whole life ahead of him, but he didn't because of the actions of two other people. Kevin was an innocent child of only fourteen years of age.

When Serena begins to investigate, it may sometimes be weeks before a small piece of information taken from the message given to her is confirmed, but she only needed one thing to match up to what she had been told or seen, then she could begin to look deeper into the whole sad story.

Serena was incredibly lucky in the way that she worked, as her sister Georgia, was always there to help her decipher information, and was always quick enough to tell her when she needed to rethink it. Georgia always said, 'Two brains are better than one,' and she was right about that. It was always good to have someone to talk to.

Serena phoned Georgia to tell her that she had a new case, and the next day Georgia called round to help. Serena had told Georgia a little bit about how all of this had come about. Georgia's first task was to ask Serena to repeat everything she remembered from the spirit message; in case she had left something out.

'Okay, Serena. Begin at the very start of the message, what you saw, heard, names and everything. How you saw it, and how you interpreted it. I'll take notes because I might interpret things differently to you.'

Serena was glad Georgia was here. She took her mind back to the very first image she saw. 'I saw a young boy. His name was Kevin.' Serena described him to Georgia. 'He was standing alone on the edge of a rocky outcrop, surrounded by hills. He began talking to me and said they'd killed him at a place called Bonfire Hill. They had chased and tormented him by throwing bottles and large rocks, and they laughed when he was hurt.' Serena looked sad. He was stabbed twice and died.'

Serena turned to Georgia. 'He died from his stab wounds and head injuries. By the sounds of things there must be two of them, because Kevin kept saying "them" when he was referring to his killers, and he gave me their first names.'

All this information was becoming a little too much for Georgia. 'I really don't know how you can cope with all of this. It's so sad.' A teardrop rolled down Georgia's face. Georgia quickly wiped it away. 'Serena, you said the name of the place was called Bonfire Hill. Have you any idea where that is?'

'No, I'm not sure, but I seem to think Kevin mentioned Cheshire. I've never heard of Bonfire Hill though. Kevin has shown me we will find his body somewhere in that area, but from what I saw in my vision, the area is vast, but all we must do is to find the rocks that he showed me.'

Georgia knew this was her cue to sit quietly while Serena read over the rest of the information.

'In the background I could see a huge bonfire. I don't know what that was supposed to mean, or if it's a cryptic clue. There were two men, around their mid-twenties, or about that. One of them was the instigator in it all, the other one followed and did what he was told. The instigator was called Tom.'

'What did the surrounding area look like? Is there any more information that you might not realise is significant?' said Georgia.

Serena thought for a while and tried to cast her mind back. 'Oh my God, yes there is. You have helped me recall something.' Serena looked excited. 'There were lots of trees close by, like a large, wooded area, and lots of buttercups everywhere.'

Georgia grabbed Serena's hand. 'That's brilliant, now you have to add that to your list.'

The sisters sat for a while and chatted about where to begin, concluding that the first thing would be to start trying to find out where Bonfire Hill is. They knew it couldn't be too far away as Serena said Kevin sounded as though he had a local accent. Serena realised Bonfire Hill could relate to a place where an organised bonfire would be held every 5th of November on Bonfire Night. This must be significant information, as she would not have been told it.

Days passed, and they had deciphered a few more of the clues, but not enough. As Serena thought it might be getting near to the time when they could physically begin searching, more information started coming through to her. A few days later she was vacuuming the living room and sensed a presence behind her. This kind of thing had happened all her life, so it was not anything for her to be frightened of. Sometimes she saw the full apparition of the spirit, and at other times only their description and words would come through her mind's eye telepathically.

She knew without turning round that it was Kevin. She could feel his sadness straight away. He was trying to tell her something – something that sounded like, 'Corsley' or 'Gorsy' Field. Once she heard the name, Kevin went away, that's when she knew she would be following the correct information, she had just misheard in the beginning.

Serena ran to her computer, leaving the vacuuming behind. Excitedly she typed 'Gorsy Field', but no information came up for that name, so she went straight to 'Gorsy Field Cheshire', knowing that's where Kevin had said he lived. Time rolled by but in the end, she found exactly what she was looking for. Serena felt so relieved that she now knew exactly where she should begin looking for Kevin. This information is most crucial to the investigation. Then she had a sudden realisation. 'That's it! I've got it. Bonfire Hill is a nickname for where Kevin can be found. Gorsy Field is the area's real name.'

Serena rang Georgia to ask her to come round so that they could work on it together. Georgia arrived ten minutes later, really looking forward to getting this problem solved. They weren't sure where to start.

'I think we might be fighting a losing battle here, think about it,' Georgia said.

Serena looked at her, not having a clue what she must be thinking.

'Right, we both know, that you know what the area looks like, but that is not good enough. What we really need to be doing is looking for the boy's name on missing persons, or see what we can find at the library, and when we find it, we will know where he disappeared from, then we can take it from there.'

Serena cupped Georgia's face in her hands, and said, 'God, it's a good job I've got you. I knew one day you would come in handy.'

They both had a good laugh at what Serena had said.

Georgia looked at Serena. Something had dawned on her. 'You do know the boy's surname, don't you? We've got nothing without that.'

'Umm, oh God, I hope so. Where are my notes?' In a panic she began shoving everything on the desk everywhere, then stopped. Holding the most important piece of paper in the air like a flag. 'See! I knew I had it somewhere! Did you really think I would misplace something as important as this? What do you think I am.'

Georgia smiled and shook her head, always remembering what a dizzy person her big sister could be.

'Here it is. His name is...'

Serena's eyes darted all over the piece of paper that she held in her hands, then, 'Ah ha! There it is. His name is Kevin Hughes.'

They both sighed with relief. Now Serena had to find out if Kevin Hughes was on the Missing Person's list. Once she had got that information, she would know that her thoughts were confirmed, he was from Gorsy Field in Cheshire.

Over the next two weeks Serena and Georgia searched through old newspapers at the library for anything they could find about Kevin Hughes. As soon as Serena saw the picture, she recognised Kevin. It was a picture Kevin's mother had supplied, according to the caption. He looked so innocent and small for his age, such a beautiful child gone forever at the hands of others. The news clip mentioned the area he had disappeared from on that tragic day many years ago. Serena had all the valuable information that she needed, and it was time to plan her trip for her and Georgia to start searching.

Serena and Georgia spent about two hours together working out a plan. Serena showed Georgia a map of where they will be going, all of this worked out from the information Serena had received, and the newspaper articles she had found.

The following weekend the big day arrived. Georgia called round to Serena's house and they both went over the directions and made sure that they did not leave any information behind. They were both feeling a little apprehensive about things, which for Serena was natural at the start of any investigation.

The weather was not on their side. It was cold and

looked as though it could rain. This was not a good sign as none of them knew what the terrain they were about to embark on was like. All Serena knew was it was going to be a very rocky area as that's what she had seen in her visions. They had packed their boots and coats and hoped for the best. They felt lucky it wasn't too far away – only about a forty-minute drive.

When they arrived at their destination, they immediately changed into their boots. They got their things together and began walking towards the area that Serena had seen in her visions.

'Does this look like the area you saw in the message?' Georgia asked.

Serena said, in a quiet voice, 'I'm not too sure yet, Georgia. I need to go further into the field to see what I can pick out. The first image I got was the trees and buttercups, but it isn't the weather for buttercups. But that's okay because I do feel as though this is the correct place. I know Kevin will be guiding us. We also need to look for two very large flat rocks on the ground. He said we must climb down them, but don't worry we won't be doing that if we think it's going to be too dangerous. If it is, we would have to rethink things.'

Georgia knew she must trust in what her sister is feeling, even if neither of them were prepared for the vast expanse of the place. Gorsy Field was surrounded by so many kinds of natural beauty with wooded areas and fields that went on for miles, with miles of rocky outcrops. The sisters had not really fathomed how large the area was on the map.

Serena put her arm around Georgia's shoulder to comfort her, feeling her sense of hopelessness about the enormity of the task ahead. 'Hey, it's okay. We need to get further into the area and begin looking for something that I can connect with my vision as proof. We are in the correct area, so let's search the woods first, if only to eliminate them. I know he can be found where the huge black rocks are. After all, we need to do what we came here for. It might take us longer than we thought, but we will get there in the end, I promise you.'

Determined not to let the cold weather stop them, they walked further and further into the wooded area. They still had plenty of daylight left but there was also a long way to go. They walked for another couple of miles and then to their delight they came to a clearing, and maybe a couple of miles in the distance were large formations of rocks.

When they first got there, they couldn't believe what they were looking at. The area went on for miles. They both turned to each other in shock and groaned at the same time. It was going to be like finding a needle in a haystack trying to find the exact rocks that Serena had been directed to. They sat down and pulled a thermos out and enjoyed a cup of tea and a good rest before carrying on with the task that lay before them.

After a rest, Serena had mixed emotions. She hoped they would soon find the rocks where Kevin was buried, the ones she would recognise by the description he had given her, but she could not shake the apprehension she was feeling.

They walked for over an hour. Georgia kept asking, 'Are we there yet?' sounding like a little child on an uncomfortable car journey.

Serena was getting a little bit angry with her going on

and on. 'Yes, I think we are. It can't be much further. You're going to have to grin and bear it for now.'

Suddenly it was as if the canopy of the trees had been lifted off and they were now back in daylight again. They walked into the clearing, in awe of the sight before them. Miles upon miles of huge rocks of strange shapes and sizes lay before them. To Serena's amazement, she recognised the three large black rocks that Kevin had described to her. It was an amazing sight. She knew exactly which ones Kevin had wanted her to go to. Tears streamed down her face.

'Look, Georgia. That's them right over there. I knew he would guide me to the right place, I told you he would.'

Georgia felt so much pride and disbelief of what her sister had made her life's purpose. The rocks looked as though they had been there for hundreds if not thousands of years, black and tall, standing side by side going hundreds of metres into the air as though they had been spewed out from the fiery depths of Mother Earth.

That was the place where Kevin was buried. There was no way she could be wrong. Everything Kevin had described to her was now right in front of her. Now Serena had to find some kind of proof. But first, they had to figure out a way to get down the rocks that were in front of them.

This was going to be a very difficult task. The rocks looked very slippery, and she was not willing to put their lives at risk by going down there just yet. What they needed to do was to try to find out more information about where the family lived and talk to them, and that was going to be an extremely challenging task.

Chapter Eleven

Serena and Georgia started looking for information on Kevin's family, hoping they could approach them with the information they had gathered. They looked in the local phone book, but Hughes was such a common name, there was no way they could call or visit everyone listed.

They returned home and revisited the library, looking at the old newspapers to see what additional information they could find. Eventually, they found the name of the area where Kevin had lived. It wasn't much, but it was enough to plan another trip.

The following Sunday, Serena and Georgia drove out to Gorsy Field again. Once there, they had decided to approach a passer-by and ask if they knew of the name Kevin Hughes and keep asking until they found someone who did.

They had been there for over an hour and had approached only two people in that time, neither of them knowing Kevin Hughes. They began to get disillusioned. They decided to have a break and have lunch at the local pub that they'd seen on the way into town.

The pub looked very welcoming. They didn't have a clue that this was the same pub Kevin's killers were at the night before his death. They ordered a drink and a sandwich, then took a seat over near the window where they could chat without being disturbed.

They sat for about twenty minutes chatting, and looking through Serena's notes, both double checking that everything in the notes tallied up with what they were seeing.

Serena also wanted to reassure herself that she was doing the right thing trying to find someone who could help them in their quest to find a relative of Kevin Hughes.

The pub was quiet, and it didn't take long before the bartender brought their food and drinks over. He was a good-looking man and seemed to be very jolly and friendly.

'Hello, ladies. I can't recall ever seeing you in here before. Are you here visiting someone then?'

'Not really,' Serena said. 'We are looking for somebody though. Maybe you could help us?'

'I will if I can. What is it you need to know?'

'We are looking for a family called Hughes. Their son was called Kevin, but he died a long time ago and the family lived near here. Do you happen to know of them?'

The bartender looked puzzled.

'No, sorry I don't. Maybe my dad does. He's owned this pub for about twenty-five years or more now. I'll go and ask him when I've got a free minute.' Then he smiled and said, 'Enjoy your lunch, and I will let you know as soon as I can.'

Serena and Georgia turned to each other and smiled.

After they had finished their sandwiches, two men approached their table. One of the men said, 'Hello, I hope you don't mind us approaching you like this but, we've been told that you are looking for the Hughes family, specifically the family of Kevin Hughes.'

Serena replied, 'Yes, can you help us with this?'

'I should think so. My name is Owen Hughes, and this is my friend Richard. Kevin was my brother. What is it you are wanting to know?'

Serena and Georgia turned to each other in amazement. Serena wasn't sure how to begin. 'Would you like to join us?' She gestured for them to sit down. 'I'm so sorry, we didn't expect things to happen like this.'

'I can imagine. We come in here quite often and the bartender is a friend of ours. He's the one that told us you were here.'

The bartender had purposely kept it to himself that he knew Richard and Owen just in case Owen didn't want to talk to some stranger about Kevin, and he was quite shocked when Owen agreed. It didn't matter, they were here now, so they may as well find out what they were wanting.

The two men sat down. Richard asked the women for their names, thinking there might be a family connection by one of them having the name Hughes too, but of course he was wrong.

Serena looked at Georgia with a look that said, 'So, what on earth should we tell them?'

Before she answered, Owen said, 'Why do you want to know about Kevin?' He was getting quite irate about the whole situation.

Richard told him to calm down.

Georgia had a look on her face that said, 'Well go on then, you're the one that's just opened this can of worms!'

Serena took a deep breath. The truth was the only way forward now. 'I'm a psychic medium, which means I receive messages from the spirit world—'

'Oh no, don't tell me you expect us to go along with that rubbish,' Owen said, cutting her off.

'If you could just hear me out. Most of the time these messages are from the victims where they are asking me to help them so I do what I can for them. All they often want is closure...'

The two men sat there and listened, not really knowing what to think.

'...and for their remains to be found and sent home to their families, so that they can say goodbye to their loved ones after many years of being missing.'

Owen did not really know what to say to that answer. Thoughts were going round in his head saying, 'How on earth does she know that Kevin has been missing for many years? And if she knows that then she probably knows that we all suspect murder as the cause of it.' He thought Serena may have just described what had happened to Kevin.

Richard stepped in. 'Are you saying you have somehow had a message from Kevin, and you think you know where he is buried?'

'Yes I am,' said Serena.

Richard turned to Owen. 'It's okay, mate. Let's hear them

out. We won't agree to anything before we've heard all they have to say,' and in a quieter voice, he said, 'plus we have your mum to think about. What would she think of this information?'

Serena noticed both men were genuinely concerned when Owen's mum was mentioned. She had to tread very carefully so as not to hurt anyone's feelings. Serena explained a bit more about how the messages come through, and the investigating she and Georgia had done to match what she'd been told.

The conversation went on for quite a while. It was now beginning to look as if they were now wanting to listen to more of what she and Georgia had to say. They had begun to accept what she was saying, even though it was a shocking surprise to hear about the information that took them to Bonfire Hill. It was this piece of information that made them understand she was telling the truth about all that she knew and what she said that Kevin had told her. Serena had said Kevin told her about Bonfire Hill, which isn't its real name, but in the end, Kevin told her the area's real name.

Serena asked the two men if they would like another drink, and Georgia accompanied her to the bar, leaving the men mulling over the whole conversation. When they returned, the men looked much more relaxed. Now everyone was at ease.

'I know that all of what has happened in this short time of us all meeting must have come as a great shock to the both of you. Owen, you mentioned your mother. Do you think it would be okay for us all to go to see her and I will tell her how all of this came about?'

Georgia thought it could be too soon to mention that sort of thing, but Owen and Richard did not seem to mind the question so much.

'I'm not too sure, Serena. While you were at the bar, Richard and I spoke about it, and to tell you the truth, Mum isn't at all well now. She is very sick. She has cancer.'

'Oh, my goodness, I'm so sorry,' said Serena.

'It's alright, you weren't to know.' Owen looked at Richard. 'But I think we are ready to listen to whatever it is you would like to do next.'

'I think we should go to where Kevin told me to look,' Serena said.

Owen and Richard were keen to go right now, but the day was getting on and it was getting too late to do anything. They arranged to meet at Bonfire Hill the following Sunday.

Chapter Twelve

Serena and Georgia arrived before Owen and Richard, so they stood around chatting about what they were going to do, both being mindful of the way they would approach going to the area where Kevin's remains could be found. It must be so hard for them both, especially for Owen, but this had to be done.

Ten minutes later the men arrived. They were all pleased to see each other again. Serena explained how far away the rocks were from where they stood, but Owen and Richard already knew where she was talking about, being familiar with the area.

Owen, pointing over to the rocks away in the distance said, in a calm and understanding voice, 'If you are talking about the tall black ones right over there, they are known to us as the Trinicles.'

Serena felt a flush of happiness. 'I can't tell you how pleased I am that you have agreed to do this.'

Owen looked relieved. 'The thing is, after all these years, this is the closest we have ever come to any potential knowledge of his whereabouts, so let's get to it. But first, we must climb down here.' He pointed to the steep drop below. 'Lucky Richard brought a couple of ropes knowing that the area could be dangerous. Once we are down there, it's just one straight walk over to them, probably take about an hour or so.'

Finally, they were all down the steep drop safely. They gathered their things together and set off on their long walk to the rocks, and sure enough, an hour later they were there. They all stood looking at each other, all of them thinking how surreal it all felt.

Serena was the first one to speak. 'In my vision I have always felt that Kevin's remains were buried to the right-hand side of the tallest rock.' Serena pointed to the one she meant. 'Now I'm standing here with you both, I feel very positive about it. Let's begin to search around this area.'

Everyone agreed. They began searching for an area to dig in, one that they felt was right for them. Serena asked how the police had conducted their search over the years.

'In a way, they hardly did anything.' Owen said. 'Well, at least that's how it seemed. About ten years ago, they told us that they won't be leading anymore searches until someone comes forward with some definitive evidence.'

No one said anything for a while, saddened by what Owen had said. Owen continued, 'The original detective, Detective Brown, took early retirement and he was the one involved in the case right from the start. Everything came to a stop when he retired, didn't it, Richard?'

The disappointment was clear on Richard's face. 'It is what it is, and there's nothing we can do about it. Let's do all we can to find something they cannot dismiss this time.'

They each chose an area close to the rocks which they

felt could yield results and put the tools they had brought with them to work.

This was such an important thing they were doing. Kevin needed to be brought home to his family so they could finally lay him to rest. They need it, and Kevin needs it, but most of all his mother needed it. She had never been fully alive since her son disappeared. She had given birth to him, held him in her arms and kissed him for the first time in the middle of his forehead, which she was told by her own mother years ago that this is called, The Mother's Blessing, as it's the very first kiss of the child's life. All those actions do not fade from memory; they are with you for life. Serena had a sense of them all through Kevin.

Then suddenly, Georgia let out a large shriek. She pulled herself up from the ground and headed to the others in some sort of panic.

'Georgie, what on earth is wrong? Have you found something?' Serena asked.

'I think so, but I don't know what it is. I was scraping away the dirt under that rock and I think it's a piece of clothing. I'm not sure what it is. Come over and have a look.'

Owen and Richard went over.

'See, look down there. It looks like something made from wool.' Serena thought it could be a piece of Kevin's clothing.

Richard bent down to try to reveal more. He began pulling and pulling, but it would not release itself, and then with one final tug he fell backwards still holding a part of it in his hand.

They all stood around Richard, each of them trying to

get as close as they could, but in the end they all came to the same conclusion.

'It looks like a piece of a woollen garment, probably a jumper,' Richard said.

They knew this wasn't enough, that they must find more. They couldn't approach the police with just a part of a woollen garment.

This small piece of clothing meant there was a good chance this area was where Kevin was. It was still a big area to cover so they decided not to concentrate on the one spot, but to continue looking around the rocks. For the next hour they found a lot of rubbish and things that had been blown there over the years, until Richard found something else.

Richard had dug something from the ground. It was about eight inches long. It turned out to be a knife, still in its leather cover.

'This find could be very significant,' said Owen. 'Why would anybody leave this behind unless it was left here on purpose to hide their guilt?' Looking towards Serena, he said, 'This must be the burial ground. Did you see a knife in your vision?'

Serena had left the details about Kevin's murder out when she had explained things. 'I'm so sorry, Owen. I really didn't want you to know exactly how he died. All of this must be so hard to hear. But yes, it's true, that's how they took his life.'

They decided the police might be able to get some kind of print from the knife, or some kind of DNA from the cover, and rather than looking for more evidence themselves, agreed to head straight to the police station.

Besides, they did not want to be left out there in the dark.

Owen was becoming anxious. 'We need to get some kind of alibi together to tell the police, as they will wonder why we we're out here.'

Serena did not want to go to the police station and tried convincing Owen and Richard to go on their own, but they did not understand why. Serena explained that if they went with them, the police would think something doesn't seem quite right.

'What do you mean, Serena? Why should they think that?' asked Richard.

'For one thing, we can't just go there saying that we just happened to come across the knife. Look at the state of it, it's obvious it's been buried for a long time. They will not believe that.' Serena took a deep breath. 'I also really don't want to let them know that it has all come from psychic information for the sake of you both. If we do, just like other times this has happened, the police will dismiss everything that we are trying to tell them. They probably won't even agree to coming out to the area to do another search and will think I'm some kind of mad person, and you won't get anywhere.'

Owen and Richard found it a bit hard to believe, but they now trusted Serena's judgement.

Serena continued, 'I don't want that to happen. You and your family have waited long enough so let's not ruin the chance we have got. Georgia and I will head off home and wait for you to ring us about what they have said.'

'What do you think we should say then, Serena?' said Richard.

'Well, I think that you must keep any knowledge of us out of it for now. Tell them that you had gone over to the rocks, like you have done many times before, because you have always wondered if Kevin was still somewhere here or around here, as that's where you all used to play as young kids.'

'I think you are right. We could just say we came back here to look around, in the hopes of finding something,' said Richard.

Finally they all agreed and walked back to their cars and said goodbye, and as they got further away Serena shouted, 'Don't forget to ring us as soon as you have spoken to them! And good luck!'

Chapter Thirteen

Owen and Richard were on their way to the police station with the items they had recovered and to hopefully prove for the final time, that they had found Kevin's burial place. On the way, they chatted about how wonderful it would be to be able to finally put Kevin to rest and how happy Brenda would be, to be able to say goodbye to her son after all these years, but deep down both knew that all their excitement could end up being for nothing if the police could not find any DNA or clues on the knife.

They walked into the police station feeling a little bit nervous now they were there. There were already a couple of people in there, so they sat and waited their turn. Fifteen minutes later they were called over to the desk.

Richard asked the desk sergeant if they could speak to whoever took over from Detective Brown as they needed to speak to him about what they had discovered.

The desk sergeant looked at them with a frown. 'There hasn't been anyone in to replace Detective Brown. But I can get you Inspecter Brown.' The sergeant winked at the lads. 'To tell you the truth, I think he missed us too much. Came back about four years ago.' Smiling, he said, 'Anyhow, I'll go and tell him you're here. What names shall I say?'

Owen and Richard were delighted to know Inspector Brown had come out of retirement. The sergeant returned and took them to the inspector's office. Inspector Brown looked much older than they thought he would, but then again, so were they.

Inspector Brown was pleased to see them both, recognising the scrawny little teenagers were now men. 'My goodness it is good to see you. Look at you both. Owen, how is your mother doing?' said Inspector Brown,

'We're so pleased to see you have come out of retirement. Things weren't the same after you left, Inspector Brown, and well done on your promotion. As for my mum, she's not too good. I'm afraid she now has cancer.'

The inspector was shocked to hear this as he had grown very fond of the family over the years. He was still saddened about the police not finding Kevin.

'We are still hoping we can bring Kevin home before anything happens to her. That's why we have come here today. Although when we decided on coming here, we didn't know that it would be you behind the desk!'

'You had better sit down and tell me what this visit is all about,' said Inspector Brown.

Owen and Richard didn't really know where to start, but they also had to keep in mind about, not mentioning Serena and Georgia.

'We found these items earlier today over near the Trinicle rocks. We are thinking it might be the spot where Kevin is.'

Richard placed the bag on the desk and took out the items with a handkerchief, hoping not to destroy any possible clues.

Inspector Brown looked in amazement at what was before him. He was especially interested in the knife. He asked if they had taken the knife out of its case, and thankfully they hadn't. He wasn't as excited about the garment.

'I don't think that this could be of any use to us,' he said. Turning it over, dirt fell onto his desk. He wiped his hands on a tissue to get rid of the dirt. 'This could be a piece of a garment that had blown in from anywhere.'

The two men looked at each other knowing they had more to add on that subject, but not being able to say it. They were both beginning to feel a little bit disillusioned.

Richard said, without thinking, 'The fabric wasn't on the surface or sitting there with loose dirt on top of it, it was buried like the knife, and it was found in the same place as the knife. Now why would someone bother burying any kind of clothing along with a weapon? It looked to us like someone is guilty of something. The only reason these two items were buried in the same place is because someone does not want them found, and they have obviously been there for a long time. For all we know, there could be many more clues out there, and maybe even a body.'

Inspector Brown saw the look on their faces and said, 'Look, we must think about it rationally. These two items could have been there for any number of reasons. Alone, there is nothing to say that the place could be a burial site.'

'Yes,' said Richard, 'but there's also a chance that the knife could be a murder weapon. But none of us will ever know unless the police do something about checking it out.'

Inspector Brown agreed. He asked them to tell him all the details. Richard told the inspector about the times he used to play there with Kevin and their other friends, when Owen was too young to be with them.

'Well, we all used to go there on what we called an expedition. To tell you the truth, we were only about twelve years old when we first started going. In fact, I don't think any of us could even say the word 'expedition' properly. We went there many times, and we would all take a sandwich and some water and have a brilliant time. We stopped going after Kevin went missing. It wasn't the same anymore.'

Inspector Brown could see the emotion on Richard's face. 'Listen, lads. I really can't tell you an answer now, I must speak to my superiors. I can't decide on this off my own back, but one thing that is leading me to do this, is because of your Mum, Owen. I have never forgotten the look on her face each time I called round to your house, she would immediately think when she saw me walk in, that I had brought her the news she wanted, but I was never able to do that for her. I will always remember that look.'

Owen was saddened to hear this. He also knew he had to make the inspector realise how sick his Mum really was. Looking towards Inspector Brown, with a pleading look on his face, Owen said, 'You are the only one that can help us, you see. I know I told you she has cancer, but we don't think she will last much longer. She really isn't doing too well. The only thing she wants before she dies is for Kevin to come home. I'm worried that she may not get her wish.'

Inspector Brown understood. 'I'll tell you what I'll do for you,' he said.

Owen and Richard sat up and listened to what he had to say.

'I'll take these items to my superior in the hopes he will agree to having them checked out, but I cannot promise you anything. I'll also tell him how you came about them. Leave me your phone number, Owen, and I'll call you when I get a response. It could take quite a while so do not expect anything tomorrow, you must give me time on this.'

Owen and Richard couldn't have been more pleased. At last, they might be on their way to getting the help they have wanted for years.

Inspector Brown walked them to the door. 'I want you to know, Owen, that I have never forgotten about this case. It's been with me for many years, and I have never forgotten about the way both of your parents were devastated when Kevin disappeared. I truly hope that the items you have brought me can get examined and will yield some results.'

The two men knew that every word that he'd spoken was sincere, and this put their minds at ease.

Richard turned to Inspector Brown, and said, 'We are so pleased you are back here. We couldn't believe it when the desk sergeant said it was you.'

Owen added, 'I can't wait to get home to Mum and tell her you are back. She'll be overjoyed, I know she still remembers you.'

They both left feeling relieved that everything had gone this well. Now it was just a matter of time before they hear anything from Inspector Brown, and they both felt as though he was sincere about wanting to do his best.

This, up to now, had been the most positive thing that they had heard in years.

On the way back to the car, Owen called Serena to tell her how things had gone. 'Serena, you'll never guess. We got to see Inspector Brown, the detective that was on Kevin's case from the beginning. He's now back working there, and he is going to do all he can to help us once his superiors give him the go ahead.'

'Oh, that's wonderful,' Serena said. 'Maybe you'll feel more comfortable now he's back on the case. I truly hope you get an answer from him as soon as possible. What did he say about our findings?'

'We don't think he was very impressed about them. The first thing he said was, "I hope you didn't take the knife out of its case", which thankfully we didn't, and he thought both the items could have been there for many reasons, but all we can do is to hope and pray that he gets permission to reopen the case, which as you know is now classed as a cold case, I can't wait to get back home to tell Mum. Maybe this will give her a new lease of life.'

'Did he say how long things might take?' Serena asked.

'He couldn't really speculate on that. I suppose we'll all have to sit and wait. I promise that as soon as we hear anything we will call you. Just think, if we hadn't met you two the other week, none of this would be happening. And, with Inspector Brown back again, what a brilliant day this has been.'

They said their goodbyes and they drove to Owen's mums. He was so excited about getting back to his Mum's house to tell her about 'Detective' Brown, which was the name that she would remember him by.

On the drive to Owen's mum's house, Owen seemed to have a change of heart about telling her about what today had brought. 'Listen Rich, I've been thinking. I'm not sure if we should be telling Mum about this. It could be too soon. Maybe we should wait until we've heard back from Inspector Brown? Could you imagine what it would be like for her, sitting every day waiting for an answer from the police, none of us know how long all of this could take? I think we should wait until at least we know that they are going to get onto the case again, don't you?'

Richard thought for a moment. 'I suppose you're right, Owen. I never thought of that. We have both been so excited about all the positive things that have happened today, maybe we got a bit too carried away with it all.'

'Yeah, we'll hold on a bit longer, but let's still call to see her anyway.'

When they arrived, Owen used his door key. He opened the door and shouted, 'It's only me and Richard, Mum.'

Brenda was in the living room. She was now living downstairs as it was easier for her to get around to the kitchen and bathroom. As soon as they walked in there was a big smile on Brenda's face, she was always happy to see them both. Owen bent down to give her a kiss on her cheek and Richard sat next to her and held her hand. They were both still excited about what today had brought into their lives, but their decision was final, they were not going to mention it to her.

Owen asked her if she would like a cup of tea and a sandwich, and she said yes. He was less worried about her these days. She could make her own breakfast in the morning and Owen always called to see if she needed any shopping. He would also call to say good-night every evening.

Brenda's two work friends called in often to have a good chat. In between times, Brenda was on her own, so now was the time for Owen to move back in with her, that way he could spend more time with her knowing that she is alright when he was around.

She rarely went out anymore, but sometimes sits in the garden if the weather is nice. Since her cancer diagnosis she has lost quite a bit of weight and hair, due to the treatment, but overall, she was still happy in her own little world.

Chapter Fourteen

A month had passed by and Owen and Richard still had not received an answer from Inspector Brown. They were beginning to get a little frustrated. One day on his way home from work, Owen called into the police station hoping to see Inspector Brown.

Two minutes later the desk sergeant took him through to his office. Inspector Brown told Owen to take a seat.

Before Inspector Brown could say anything else, Owen said, 'Well, it's been over a month now since we came to see you about reopening the case, and we were wondering why we haven't had a response?'

Inspector Brown looked at Owen. 'Just one second please, Owen. I'll be back in a moment.'

Inspector Brown went out of the room and Owen was left there alone wondering if due to his reaction, the news was not going to be good. When Inspector Brown returned the first words out of his mouth were, 'I'm very sorry Owen but...'

Owen's first thought was, 'Here we go, excuse after excuse,' but he was pleasantly surprised.

'It's going to be a while longer yet; we haven't had the results on the items. They should be back sometime this week, and as soon as I get them, I will let you know.'

Owen felt so much better. At least it wasn't a definite 'No, we are not taking it any further.'

Owen couldn't wait to ring Richard to tell him what had been said, knowing that it would make his day. At this stage he didn't want to tell Serena and Georgia, he wanted to hang on and hopefully give them the good news that they have all been waiting for once the results were in. After all, if it hadn't been for them, none of this would be happening.

The rest of the week seemed as if it was never going to end, every minute of every day they waited for that most important phone call, but it did not come. Eventually Owen rang Serena and invited her and Georgia to the same pub they had met weeks previous for the first time. He wanted to inform them of where they are up to and thank them for their help, even if there was no new information.

Serena accepted. She realised both Owen and Richard would be feeling very disillusioned and sick and tired of waiting. They arranged a time for the following Sunday. They were all pleased to see each other and ordered lunch and a drink, and of course the topic of conversation was the police, until suddenly everything got too much for Owen.

'I've had enough of all this,' Owen said, suddenly.

They were all shocked.

'Why can't the police do what they say? Why is it they tell you one thing, then don't stick to what they tell you?' Owen put his head in his hands in despair. 'All I want is my brother back, this is the one and only chance. You would think they would at least stick to what they have said.'

Richard had not seen Owen in such a state for a long time. He put his arm around Owen's shoulders. 'Listen, Owen. If we haven't heard anything in the next few days, we'll get back in touch with Inspector Brown and ask what's going on. Bear in mind that we can at least thank these two ladies here,' he gestured to Serena and Georgia, 'because if it wasn't for them, we wouldn't even be this close. If Serena hadn't seen the area in her vision, and we hadn't found the items when we went to that area, then we wouldn't even be this far, would we?'

Owen nodded his head in agreement,

'So, for now, we must sit and pray that when the news comes it is going to be good news. Now it's time we went to see your mum. She will be expecting you, since it is weekend.'

Owen had listened to every word that Richard said, and he agreed with him.

As they got up to leave, Owen asked Serena and Georgia if they would like to come and see Brenda, to which they said a very eager yes. When they arrived at Brenda's, Owen unlocked the front door and walked in first, so that he didn't frighten his mum. She was sitting up in bed in the living room watching television.

'Hello Mum, it's me and Richard, and we have brought some people to see you, I hope you don't mind.' Brenda turned to look at him. Owen had to raise his voice as Brenda was now a little hard of hearing. 'These are two friends of ours, they have come to say hello to you on their way past. We have been for a drink at the pub, and they asked how you were, so I invited them round. I hope you don't mind,' Owen pointed over to them. 'This is Serena, and this is her sister, Georgia.'

Brenda turned to look at the women. 'Oh hello,' she said. 'Who are you again? I can't remember your names.'

'It's okay, Mum, you haven't met them before. I'm going to make us all a cup of tea. Would you like one, Mum?'

Owen invited Serena and Georgia to sit down while he went to make the tea. Richard sat next to Brenda, chatting to her. When Owen returned with the tea, Serena was sitting on one side of Brenda and Georgia on the other, with Richard now watching TV. They were sitting chatting to each other as if they had been friends for years.

Serena suddenly noticed something from the corner of her eye. It was a photograph of Kevin on the top of the television, and by the looks of things it must have been taken not long before he disappeared.

Serena's mind began to wander back to the vision that she had seen of him. It was so clear it felt like it was happening all over again. She could sense that Kevin was with her, but of course she could not tell anyone else. She felt honoured right at this moment to be in the house with his family.

Everyone was having an enjoyable time, chatting, and laughing together, until suddenly Owen's phone rang. It was Inspector Brown. Owen gestured to Richard to follow him into the kitchen. Finally! It was the news they had been waiting for.

The police had got DNA from the knife, and it was a match to Kevin as well as Thomas Hughes. They had decided to reopen the case based on the evidence they had found and would organise an official search of the area around the Trinicles for Kevin's remains.

The tears ran down Owen's face. He could not hold them back. Owen and Richard were too emotional to go back into the living room, they could not allow Brenda to see them in that state. They had to calm themselves down, so they went out into the garden.

After about ten minutes, Serena knew there was something going on that had started with the phone call. Serena gestured to Georgia that she was going into the kitchen.

When Serena realised Owen and Richard were no longer there, she opened the back door to see if they were in the garden. Before she could ask anything, Owen turned to her and hugged her. He could not let go; tears were streaming down his face.

Still sobbing, he said, 'Serena, you're not going to believe it. The phone call was from Inspector Brown. They are going to open the case again. Oh my God, my heart is pounding. I really need to sit down I just can't believe that my brother could finally be coming home.'

Serena helped him to the kitchen so that he could sit down and stayed with him until he had calmed down a little, then she left Owen and Richard alone to discuss their next move, which was deciding if they should tell Brenda. They had to tell her something as Brenda, even in her confused state, she still seemed to know something was going on. They would have to tell her at least about the police reopening the case.

Slowly, the living room door opened, and Owen and Richard walked in. Owen sat next to his Mum on the bed, then he gently took hold of Brenda's hand. She looked up to him somehow knowing that he had something important that he wanted to say, but she didn't have a clue what it could be. Serena and Georgia had moved away from the bed so that Richard could join Owen in talking to Brenda.

'Mum, I have something to tell you.'

Brenda looked towards Owen.

'Can you recall how long it has been since we lost Kevin? And all the years that you have prayed for him to come home to us?' said Owen.

Brenda understood exactly what he was saying but it wasn't sinking in.

'Mum, do you remember Kevin disappeared a long time ago? Well, do you recall that nice policeman that used to come to let us know how the search for him was going, his name was Detective Brown?'

Brenda nodded, tears forming in her eyes. It was as if she had instantly recalled the name.

'He has just told me on the phone that they are going to go out searching for Kevin again, because they think they know where his body might be found, and these two ladies here,' he gestured towards Serena and Georgia, 'well, they are the ones that have found where he might be.'

'My Kevin is coming home to me? I've waited for him for such a long time. Do you think he will be home tonight?'

It was the kind of comment Owen was dreading because it showed how Brenda was no longer seeing the whole picture, how she no longer understands everyday life, but understands the past. That was the main reason he and Richard hesitated about giving her the news after the phone call from 'Detective' Brown.

Now the only thing to do was to wait, none of them knowing just how long.

Chapter Fifteen

A week later, when Owen was at work, he was told he had an urgent phone call at the office. To his surprise it was Inspector Brown.

'Oh, hello, Inspector Brown. I wasn't expecting to hear from you today. Please don't give me any bad news.'

'No, I won't, Owen, I have good news for you. We have found human remains at the search site.'

There was silence from Owen for a few seconds. 'I'm so sorry, Inspector Brown. I'm so used to waiting and then not getting the answer that I have waited for every day. I can't believe what you have just said. Is it Kevin?'

'At the moment all we know is that there have been human remains found at the search site. For now, we don't have any idea who the remains belong to until there has been further DNA testing.'

'When do you think we will get an answer? How long will it take?'

'I'm not too sure. Maybe a couple of days. Come to think of it, with all the new technology they have out there these days, it could even be hours, but don't hold me to that. I will be in touch as soon as I can.'

Owen's manager had heard most of the phone conversation, and knowing about the situation of the family, he told Owen to leave work straight away and get home to his mum. On his way to the car, Owen called Richard and told him the good news. Richard said he would be round as soon as he could get off from work.

Richard arrived a few hours later. Brenda was sleeping so they decided to go into the kitchen to talk so as not to disturb her. They both sat down, still buzzing from the excitement. Brenda was completely oblivious to the huge development that was going on around her.

Richard suddenly thought about something. 'Owen, have you decided to tell your mum about the development, are you going say something to her now?'

'No Richard, I haven't had a chance yet. I think it's best if we keep it quiet for now, due to the reaction that she gave a while ago when we told her about the case being opened again. If you remember she thought he would be home that night, and then she never mentioned it again. I don't really think she can think in the present anymore, and she is sleeping a lot, due to the increase in her cancer medication.'

'Yes, I think you're right, Owen. Anyhow I think it's time we went back into check on her. Oh, don't you think we should ring Serena and Georgia to tell them the good news?'

'Yes, we should. Let's go back in the other room and I will ring her now.'

Serena answered the phone. 'Oh, hello, Owen. How are things going? Have you heard anything yet?'

'Yes, we have, Serena. I've had a phone call to say that human remains have been recovered, we are so excited. But they don't know if they belong to Kevin.'

Serena gasped. 'Oh, my goodness! That's such amazing news, but all I can say is that I wouldn't have been told about that area from Kevin if it wasn't the correct area, or otherwise how could I have led you there? I suppose all we can do for now is to hope and pray that the remains are Kevin's, but they can't be confirmed until the results come back from pathology. Is that right, Owen?'

'Yes, that's right, Serena. I suppose I am just so worried that it might not be him. Richard and I were wondering if you and Georgia would like to meet up at the pub again tomorrow and we can all have lunch together, that's if we have calmed down by then, because now Richard is just as bad as I am!'

Serena laughed. 'Sounds brilliant. We would love to. I can't believe what you have just told me, I am thrilled to bits for you.'

'Good, shall we say about one pm, if that's okay with you?'

'Perfect, we will see you then. Oh, Owen, how's your mum doing?'

'Oh, she's fine now. She doesn't say or do much anymore, but she's fine.'

'That's good. We are so looking forward to seeing you all. See you tomorrow.'

The following day was Sunday and still no news from Inspector Brown. Owen settled his mum down and when she was comfortable, he called round to ask a neighbour if she would keep a check on her, then he went to meet the others at the pub.

When he arrived, they were all pleased to see each other, and of course the topic of conversation was the discovery of human remains. The conversation was going along fine at first or so they all thought, but then, Owen became quite upset about the whole thing and said, 'I just don't understand why we haven't heard anything else from Inspector Brown yet. I had it in my mind that by the time we all met up here I would have some brilliant news for you all, that the remains found are Kevin's. But no, not a thing.'

They all looked at one and other and could feel the hurt that Owen must be feeling.

Richard, knowing that it takes a lot for Owen to get so upset, suggested going back to the house.

'That's a good idea, Richard, then Serena and Georgia can see Mum again,' Owen said.

They arrived at the house and Owen opened the door. He went inside, and his mum was awake, but she hadn't heard him.

'It's only me, Mum,' Owen called out. 'Richard and some other friends want to see you.'

Once they were all inside, Owen introduced Serena and Georgia to Brenda again, knowing that she had probably not got any recollection of them whatsoever. She looked up at them and smiled.

Brenda said, 'Hello, who are you?'

'Mum, I have told you their names once, have you forgotten again?' Owen said grinning. 'This is Serena, and this is Georgia. They have come to chat to you for a while, so would you like me to make you a cup of tea and a sandwich?'

Owen looked towards Richard who was smiling at what

Brenda had just said, knowing that it is the kind of thing that happens often. Minutes later, Serena was sat on a chair at one side of the bed, and Georgia at the other. They were chatting and laughing about all sorts of things that Brenda probably didn't understand but giggled along with them anyway. Richard went to help Owen.

Another hour passed by, and it was time for Serena and Georgia to leave, they couldn't hang on any longer for the all-important phone call that didn't come. They went over to Brenda to say goodbye to her, and Owen stood up to show them out.

Owen opened the front door, and to everyone's surprise, Inspector Brown was standing there just about to ring the doorbell. He had a colleague with him, and Owen invited them both inside. Serena and Georgia also went back inside, hoping to hear good news.

Owen said, 'Inspector Brown, please tell me that you have come to tell us about some good news at last. Please come in and sit down.'

'Thank you, Owen, yes, we are pleased to tell you that the DNA results have come back as a positive match for your brother Kevin.'

Owen was so shocked he slumped down into a chair and cried. Richard went over to him straight away to console him, both feeling the joy and the sadness of the words that have just been said to them. The words that they have waited for, for so many years.

Serena and Georgia just stood in shock at what they had all just been told.

Owen's sadness all poured out. At losing a brother that he loved, and having to see his parents go through the agony and upset that nearly tore them apart, Richard having to go through the upset of losing his best mate and blaming himself for leaving Kevin alone to have to face the two people that murdered him, one of them being his own half-brother.

Owen looked towards Brenda, realising that she must be wondering what was going on, so he went over to her and knelt on the floor beside her, holding her hands, and said, 'Mum, these two people are here to bring us some good news.'

Brenda looked at Owen, somehow knowing that Owen and Richard were upset about something.

'They are here to tell us that Kevin is coming home to us, they have found Kevin's body, and now we will be able to send him to Heaven to be with Dad.' Owen hoped he was saying words that she would hopefully understand. 'Would you like that, Mum?'

Owen was shocked at what Brenda said next.

'My Kevin is coming home to me at last, that's good, and your dad as well. I can see them both now, can't I? I haven't seen them for such a long time. I've missed them both so much.'

Richard heard the comment Brenda had made and saw the look on Owen's face. Inspector Brown and his colleague stood in silence, watching as so many people suddenly had the closure that they had all waited for. It was a very emotional time for all of them.

Eventually, Owen looked towards Inspector Brown and realised that he was still there. He and Richard walked over to him to thank him for all he had done.

Owen gestured towards Serena and Georgia and said,

'By the way, Inspector Brown. These two ladies here,' and he pointed to Serena and Georgia, 'are the ones that led us to the place where you have found Kevin's remains. This is Serena, and this is her sister Georgia. Serena is a psychic medium, and she receives messages from spirit and her angels to ask for her help in finding the remains of cold case victims. If it wasn't for these two ladies, Kevin would still be out there on his own. Now, thanks to them, we can have him back to put him to rest, which is all any of us has ever wanted.'

Inspector Brown looked shocked at what had just been said. He really didn't know what to say, but he and his colleague looked very surprised but maybe for professional reasons, they knew that it would be best not to comment.

Owen was just about to open the front door to show Inspector Brown and his colleague out when he heard a commotion going on outside. Opening the door, there were three reporters outside, all shouting questions so loudly that nobody could understand what was being said. Owen didn't know what to do or say, but he soon realised that they must have heard about Kevin's remains being found.

He looked towards Inspector Brown as if to say, 'Please get rid of them.'

Inspector Brown moved forward, took out his police identification and there was sudden silence. He turned towards Owen and Richard. 'If you have any questions about anything, just call me at the station.'

The reporters all moved on soon after that.

The following morning, Owen woke up still anxious after a very stressful night of tossing and turning. He was worrying about all sorts of things, mainly about having to organise a funeral for Kevin once pathology had done their job.

Owen had never had to do anything like this in his life before and didn't really know where to begin. Thankfully, he knew Richard would always be there to help him, but then, he remembered what Inspector Brown had said just before he left the previous day. He told him to contact him if he needed any help or advice.

Owen had spent most of the morning thinking about things and at the same time making sure that his mum was alright. First, he helped her to get washed and dressed and then settled her down in bed so that she could have her breakfast, which she hardly touched.

Once satisfied that she was settled watching television, Owen called Inspector Brown. He needed some advice. He was put through to Inspector Brown straight away.

'Oh, hello, Owen. What can I do for you? Is everything alright? I hope those reporters haven't been bothering you again.'

'No, it's nothing like that, Inspector Brown. I was just wondering about something, and I was hoping you could help me with it,' said Owen.

'Well yes if I can. What is it?'

'I need to know how long Kevin's remains will be allowed to be kept at the morgue.'

'They are normally allowed to be kept at the morgue for up to twenty-one days, once the police have done their part. Then the coroner is free to release the remains, at which time the family should have investigated the funeral arrangements.'

'Thank you, Inspector Brown. Do you think I should get onto an undertaker soon then?'

'Yes, I do, Owen. I think that would be best. He will be the one that will liaise with the coroner's office for you. Just let me know if you need anything else.'

'Will do. And thank you again for all your help.'

Soon after, Owen began to look for an undertaker. He had so much to take into consideration and sadly, Brenda wasn't in any kind of mental state to be able to help him. Eventually he found one that he was satisfied with, so he told him the situation of Kevin's remains being recovered, and the undertaker gave him a few dates where he was available, but of course everything depended on when the remains would be released by the coroner.

Owen had only just finished on the phone, when he heard a loud commotion going on outside. He opened the front door and to his shock horror the reporters were back again. Then he noticed one of his neighbours talking to one of them. He was absolutely horrified. The only thing he could do, so as not to encourage them into asking him any questions, was to go back inside straight away, knowing by the look on the neighbour's face, she had probably innocently, answered anything they had already asked her.

Now the news of Kevin being found was soon going to be all over the morning newspapers, and there was nothing he could do about it. Owen rang Richard and told him what had happened. Richard called round to be with Owen and Brenda as soon as he could and stayed with them until the evening.

The next morning Owen heard the newspaper getting

delivered, and he quickly went to pick it up. There it was on the front page, the whole sad story of his brother's disappearance, dredged up from years ago, including an image of Thomas Hughes with a photo of him finally being arrested after so long on the run, and Simon Patterson. To Owen it still seemed like everything had happened yesterday. Sadly, these are the kind of stories that sell newspapers.

For days afterwards, there were sympathy cards and letters being pushed through the letter box, most of them had small amounts of money inside them, to go towards the funeral costs.

Owen was totally overwhelmed with the love and compassion shown by people from all around, but the person he could and would always rely on was Richard. He knew he was always at the end of a phone if he needed him, and at this moment in time, he did.

Chapter Sixteen

Owen had begun to see a change in his mum. She used to be quite easy to take care of but now he was starting to get worried about her as she was becoming very difficult. He had begun to suspect that the change started after him telling her that Kevin's remains had been found, and that because of her mental state, she didn't know how to deal with it.

One minute she would try to have a conversation with him, always about something trivial mainly from her past, and at other times, she would just sit and cry. When he tried to console her, she would push him away, but that would never stop him from giving her the best attention he could and making her comfortable for the time she had left.

It was getting late, so Owen kissed his mum goodnight before retiring to bed himself, as he was feeling emotionally exhausted from what he had to deal with during the day. The following morning Owen cleared away the breakfast dishes and made sure that Brenda was settled down, when his phone rang. It was the undertaker, Mr Collins.

'Oh, good morning, Mr Collins. This is an early call. Have you got good news for me?'

'Yes, I have, Owen. I've called to let you know that the

coroner has now released Kevin's remains to the morgue and I have received the necessary paperwork, so when you are ready, we can begin to make funeral arrangements.'

Owen was so pleased and rang Richard and Serena, straight away. They were all thrilled about the news, especially Serena. It was so good to hear that a spirit that had come to her for help, had been recovered, and can now be put to rest.

Richard could not wait to be able to finish his shift at work, so that he could go round to see Owen, and particularly Brenda. He could just imagine how excited Brenda was going to be if she understood, but this news will hopefully help her to feel better, and maybe even bring her mind back, if only a little bit, to the way she once was. But this was all just a thought and a wish. Richard arrived at the house, Owen answered the door to him, they were so pleased to see each other, because they knew that after all these years things were finally coming to an end.

They could now put the brother and friend that they had loved and missed for so many years to rest, once the funeral director gives them a date, but he did tell Owen that he will do all he could to get it earlier rather than later, which would give Owen extra time to make final arrangements with family and friends.

Now it was time for Owen to tell his mum about all what was going on, hoping that she would understand. Owen and Richard sat either side of Brenda's bed both holding her hands. Brenda sat smiling at them, as they were the only two people that she always recognised, apart from Detective Brown.

Owen was looking down at her hand as he held it in his. When he looked up to her, she was smiling at him with tears in her eyes, as if she somehow knew what he was going to say. Then she looked towards Richard, the person who had been in her life for what seemed like forever, the one who had always been a good friend to her beautiful son that she missed so deeply.

Owen gently turned her face towards her and said, 'Mum, I need to tell you something and I want you to listen very carefully to what I am going to say.'

She looked towards Richard and then back towards Owen. It was as if she knew something was going on but because of her declining health, she did not have the ability to comment on it. Owen continued in a low voice that was filled with emotion.

'Mum, listen to me. Kevin is coming home. We can now have a funeral for him, and he can get to be with the angels, where he will be safe and happy with dad. Do you understand what I am telling you?'

Brenda just looked at him for a few seconds and said, 'Oh yes, I do. I would like to see them both again, do you think they will be here soon?'

Then she turned towards Richard and said the same, both feeling that she knew what had been said to her but did not fully comprehend it. Brenda then sat holding their hands for a few more minutes, without saying another word, then she lay back and went to sleep.

Richard stayed for another couple of hours. Neither he nor Owen knew if Brenda really understood what she had been told, but just talking about the present situation they both felt that she did, and that is all they could hope for. Richard left telling Owen that he will see him in the morning.

Owen made his mum her night-time cocoa and he sat with her for a while. Then he made sure she was comfortable, and laid her down to sleep for the night, and went to bed himself.

The next morning Owen woke at around nine o'clock, which was unusual for him, as he is normally up and out for work by seven, then after a bit of a panic he realised it was Saturday. His mind had been so mixed up with all that had been going on.

He opened his bedroom door and listened to see if he could hear his mum making a noise, or even snoring like she did do most nights, but he could not hear anything unusual, so he set about getting himself showered and dressed ready to start the day in a positive way.

He went downstairs and opened the living room door quietly to check on her. He walked over to her bed, and she was fast asleep smiling about something, he pulled the covers over her to make sure she was warm enough, then he went into the kitchen to make them both breakfast.

When it was ready, he took it into her. He placed it down on a small table nearby and went over to wake her, that was when he noticed that Brenda's breathing did not sound quite right. He rang for the doctor to come out to see her straight away.

The doctor was there within fifteen minutes. He took one look at Brenda, and he knew that she had had a heart attack, possibly because of her reduced immune system due to the cancer. She would be a very lucky woman if she survived it. He called for an ambulance straight away.

While they were waiting for the ambulance to arrive, Owen went upstairs to pack her a few things that she would need for her stay in hospital. Owen was panicking so much that he was no longer able to think straight. He began looking for her slippers, completely forgetting that she already had them at the side of her bed downstairs. Then suddenly he heard the doctor calling for him to come down.

Owen shouted down, 'I won't be long doctor; I'm just looking for—'

'No, it doesn't matter about them, Owen. I need you down here now please.'

Owen walked back into the living room, and he immediately sensed that there was a problem.

'I am deeply sorry, Owen, but your mother has already passed. I am so sorry to have to tell you this. There was nothing I could do to help her.'

Owen looked at the doctor, knowing that he was speaking to him, but he could not hear the words that came from his mouth. He was in shock; the words were there but they would not come out. He sat down on the edge of the bed, holding his mum's hand, he began to cry silently, not knowing what to say or do, but he knew there was nothing more that could be done.

The doctor walked over to Owen to check if he was okay. Owen raised his head, and the doctor said to him, 'I am so sorry, Owen, but your mum was an extremely sick lady, and as I was holding her, she was just staring, smiling, as if she could see something, then she said the name Kevin. I thought she meant you at first, then I remembered you are, Owen. I think some patients, just before they pass must think of a loved one that was remarkably close to them like your brother was, I recall seeing other patients do the same thing.'

Owen was shocked at what the doctor had just said, but he did not comment on it.

There was a knock on the door. It was the paramedics, but they now needed an undertaker instead. The doctor went over to speak to them and explained that the patient had just passed away.

They left soon afterwards, and the doctor wrote out a death certificate, which now means that the undertaker that Owen had in mind to do Kevin's funeral, is needed to do Brenda's also, and he had to be called to organise taking Brenda to the hospital mortuary.

This had been the moment Owen had dreaded for many years. What will he do without his beautiful Mum, who had loved and cared for him all his life.

The doctor sat down next to him and asked if there was someone that he could contact for him, so that he would not be alone once the body had been taken away. Owen gave him Richard's number and he was there within ten minutes.

Owen was still sitting on the bed when Richard arrived. Richard went over to Owen to console him, as Owen stood up to greet him. By this time, the undertakers had arrived and were speaking to the doctor. The doctor explained the situation that had occurred, and that a death certificate had been issued.

The undertakers were now preparing themselves, ready to take Brenda out to the vehicle. They placed Brenda's body onto a stretcher, and Owen and Richard could do nothing but watch as she left them and her home for the final time.

Owen knew that he must speak to the undertakers about having a double burial, and he told Richard his plan. Richard agreed with everything Owen had suggested.

When the undertakers came back inside, Owen approached them and spoke to them about it. 'Would it be possible to arrange a double burial with you, as I would like Kevin and Mum to be together.'

'Yes, I'm sure we can do that for you, and I am so terribly sorry for your loss, but having them buried together is a wonderful idea. I will do all I can to help you. Maybe you would like to come to the office when you feel ready and I will show you some information, on what you might find is suitable for this situation.'

All Richard could do now was to make sure that he was there for Owen. The doctor stayed a little while longer to give them instructions on what Owen should do next, and then he left.

The next thing Owen saw was his beautiful Mum being carried by the undertakers out to their vehicle.

Owen and Richard were now left alone, knowing that Brenda never got the chance she had waited many years for, of seeing her son being brought home to her, so that he could be given a funeral of his own, and finally be laid to rest.

Richard decided that it would be best for him to stay with Owen that night, he thought he was too upset to be left there on his own. There was so much that needed to be discussed and organised, but Owen was not in any fit state just yet, he really did not know where to begin.

The hours were dragging by, and yet nothing had been put into perspective. The next thing Richard knew was that Owen had fallen asleep on his mum's bed.

The following morning Owen awoke to total silence in the house. He sat up in bed knowing that everywhere felt different to him, then he realised where he was, which is when everything came rushing back into his mind.

Recalling the upset of the previous day when he had to see his beautiful loving Mum who had suffered so much waiting for years for Kevin to come home, being taken out of the house by two strangers, the image will stay with him for many years. He lay back down trying to find the motivation to get off the bed, but he had so much going round and round in his head he could barely think properly.

Richard had by this time woken up also, so he got up and went downstairs. The first thing he saw was Owen lying on his mother's bed, he had been there all night. At that moment he knew he had to help Owen to begin the day organising everything that needed to be done, he really was not looking forward to doing any of it. Richard gently tapped Owen on his shoulder to see if he was awake.

Owen was pleased to see that Richard was still there; he was the only person that had been in his life near enough since the day he was born and after losing Kevin he became like a brother to him.

Richard could see that Owen was struggling with the emotion of what had happened, so he went to make him a cup of tea. When Richard walked back into the living room, Owen was wiping the tears away from his eyes.

Richard then offered him the tea. 'There, you go, mate. Hopefully this will make you feel a bit better.'

'I really don't think anything could, I just feel as though Mum could walk back in through the front door at any moment. God, I'm going to miss her so much.'

Richard saw the look of so much sadness on Owen's face, and said, 'I know you are, Owen, and so will I. She was a lovely kind lady and had suffered so much over the years, but the thing is that you now must begin organising the funeral and putting all her affairs in order.'

'I don't think I can face all that just yet, Rich. I feel sick to my stomach, I just don't know where to begin.'

'That's why I'm here to help you. Come on, drink your tea before it gets cold, then we will put our heads together and sort things out.'

They both sat quietly for a while, Richard knowing that Owen needed a few minutes to think.

Owen looked at Richard and said, 'Well, come on then, we need to get things sorted. Where do you suggest we begin?'

Richard was shocked at Owen's sudden enthusiasm. 'You start sorting things out with the undertaker and I will start taking the bed back upstairs for you.'

Three hours had passed by. Owen had spoken to the undertaker, and he had to wait for him to get back to him with a date. During that time Richard had cleared the bed away and tidied up around the living room, so he suggested that they go to the pub for lunch hoping that Owen would agree.

Owen did agree, knowing that it was not doing him any good sitting in the house constantly thinking about his Mum and Kevin, plus there was still so much to sort out and at least Richard was there to help him.

Richard got their drinks from the bar and went to sit down with Owen. As he was walking over to him, Richard could see that Owen was in a world of his own, as though he did not know what to think or do next.

Richard sat down next to him, and they began to talk about their plans of what relatives or friends to ring next, to tell them that Brenda had passed away. Had she left a will, and the list went on and on.

Then some friends of Owen's went over to speak to them, 'Hello, Owen, how are you? We just thought that we would come over to say how pleased we are that your brother's remains have finally been found. It's been such a long time. We are so sorry to hear about your Mum. Please know that we are here for you if you need anything. At least now you can put them both to rest together.'

Owen said, 'Thank you so much. Yes, it has been far too long, we are just sitting here trying to sort all the arrangements out.'

Saying goodbye, the couple left them alone, realising that they were busy. Owen turned to Richard to say something, but he looked as though he was deep in thought. 'Richard what's wrong?

'Oh, I'm fine, Owen. I don't know if you realise it or not, but I can't believe that we haven't told Serena and Georgia about your mum yet. We should ring them when we get back to the house.'

Owen looked at Richard, surprised at what he had just said. 'I was just thinking that I will take a couple of days off work so that we can get the ball rolling on the funerals, that's if you want my help, Owen. I feel as though I could be rushing you, or maybe you would like one of your relatives to help you.'

'No, Richard I don't, I would much rather do all of this with you. Come on. It's time we got back home to ring Serena.'

When they arrived back at the house it was the first thing Owen did.

'Oh, hello, Owen,' said Serena. 'I was hoping it was you. Is everything okay, is your mum alright?'

'Well, not exactly, Serena. I'm afraid I'm ringing to tell you and Georgia that she died yesterday.'

'Oh, my goodness, I am so sorry. What was it?'

'A heart attack in the end. I can't believe all of what she went through with the cancer and then the onset of dementia, and now this.'

The phone went quiet, neither of them knew what to say.

Serena spoke first. 'Owen, is Richard with you? You shouldn't be on your own at a time like this.'

'Yes, he is, Serena. I couldn't manage to do all this without him. We have been sorting out the undertaker, he is going to do a double burial which I feel is the most fitting thing to do seeing as Mum waited so long to have Kevin back with her. So now they can both be together, thanks to you, and I know for a fact that this is what she would have wanted. In fact, I think it's what she has probably hung on for.'

'That sounds brilliant, Owen, and I agree with everything you have just said. I will go to see Georgia and tell her the sad news. Please let us know if you need any help with anything. Don't forget we are just at the end of the phone, I will speak to you soon, Owen, please know that Georgia and I will be thinking about you both.'

'I will do, Serena, thank you for being there for us. I only wish that there were more people like you and Georgia around. See you soon.'

Chapter Seventeen

Day after day cards and letters were still being posted through the letter box, and flowers were being left on the doorstep. Owen and Richard were overwhelmed by the thoughtfulness of the people around them.

Serena and Georgia arrived at the house around midday. By that time Owen and Richard had been very busy trying to decide things like what kind of coffin Owen wanted and what hymns he thought his mum would want. The list was endless. Then there was the other problem of what kind of coffin he wanted for Kevin, of course the only thing he could think of was it had to be the same as his mum's.

Money was a bit of a problem, but he would cross that bridge when he comes to it, but for now they will both receive the best he can give. They all chatted about all those things together and Owen was grateful to all of them for their approval. He was now beginning to think that he was doing his best and things were falling into place.

The next morning Owen was at home alone, sitting contemplating the whole situation, and thankful that most things had been done. There was a knock on the door. It was Richard. 'Hi, Richard, come on in, I wasn't expecting you.'

'I know you weren't, Owen.' Richard walked in.

Owen knew there was something wrong with him. 'Are you okay, mate? You don't seem yourself.'

'I'm alright, Owen, but I need to ask you something.'

'Okay, what is it?'

'I want to know if you will come for a walk to Bonfire Hill with me?'

Owen was a bit shocked at this request. 'What do you want to go there for?'

'I just feel as though I need to go.'

Owen noticed that Richard seemed to look as though he really needed to do this, so he agreed.

They set off but Richard was still quiet. When they arrived at Bonfire Hill, Richard walked straight to the area where he had last seen Kevin, on the day that he died. They both stood in silence, Richard not speaking, and Owen still wondering why he felt the need to be there. Then suddenly Richard looked up at Owen and began to cry, the crying turned into sobbing with him hardly being able to get a word out. All the time Owen was trying to console him.

They sat down and Owen asked what the problem was.

Richard said, 'I needed to come back here. This is the place where I last saw Kevin, just before he was with Tom Hughes and the other guy. Minutes later they had murdered him. I have never got over the fact that Tom Hughes was your half-brother, Owen, and because of him, Kevin has gone for ever.'

'That wasn't your fault, Rich.'

Richard looked at Owen, the tears we still streaming down his face. 'I was the one that caused all of this, it was my fault. I don't care what anybody else says, if I had stayed around, I could have helped Kevin, and he would still be with us now.'

'No, Rich, you're wrong. If you had of stayed, it wouldn't have made any difference. You two were kids, those guys were older than you and they were out for trouble that day. They would have ended up starting on some-one else anyhow, that's the type of people they were. It's all over now, Rich, both are now dead, you have nothing to be guilty about.'

Richard looked at Owen, finding it hard to comprehend what Owen has just said. 'Yes, but just look at all the heartache I caused your family. The hurt and sadness that all of you had to put up with for all these years.'

'Yeah, and just look at all the years that we all still loved you anyway! None of it was your fault! You have always been like a brother to me, and you have always been considered as part of the family.'

Richard began to feel relief. He could feel the guilt he had held in for all these years, slowly being released from his body, never to take hold of him again.

Owen had always known that if Richard had not been around for him when he was a small child, that his life would have been so much worse. Richard was always there for him when he needed him. Owen always knew that Richard could never take the place of Kevin, but after all these years there was no one else in the world that had always been there for him, to talk to him when things got tough, like when his dad died and all the other things that go on in people's families. In other words, It's the way life is. Owen knew he could not have faced it all if Richard had not been there to help him.

The day of the funerals had arrived. Owen and Richard were at the house waiting for friends, relatives and of course Serena and Georgia to arrive. They both knew that if they had not met Serena and Georgia on that day, this day would not be happening.

They sometimes sit and talk about it and neither of them will ever be able to understand how that day led to this, the day where Kevin and Brenda will finally be together. Owen reminded Richard what Serena had said to them once. That the Universe works in mysterious ways; this day was meant to happen by the coming together of the four of us, all searching for the same answer to be able to put right, what was meant to be.

All the family and close friends were sat together in the living room when Serena noticed the funeral cars arriving. The room suddenly went into total silence, and people began to slowly walk outside. The small garden was full of flowers that people had left with cards that had kind words written on them.

There were two funeral cars, the first one was for Brenda with the word TOGETHER spelt out in flowers, and the second one for Kevin with the word FOREVER also spelt out in flowers.

TOGETHER FOREVER

The matching coffins were beautiful. Then it came time for Owen to step outside. He was followed by Richard. They were both shocked to see the huge gathering of people out there. Their neighbours from the surrounding area were there and people they didn't know had come from all over to see mother and son once again united in love.

They had all heard about the recovery of Kevin's remains being found after so many years, but then the added sadness of Brenda passing, but all of them had the same thought, and that was 'how beautiful it was for them both to be buried together at the same time and in the same grave after so many years.'

There were people stood along both sides of the street, many of them bowed their heads as the cars passed them by. The main mourners got into the funeral cars for the short slow drive to the churchyard, and many people walked behind the cars.

When they arrived at the churchyard, Owen and Richard were surprised to see other people there also. They both thought this was strange as they did not recognise anyone, so they put it down to them being local people who wanted to pay their respects.

Everyone was stood around waiting for the coffins to lead them into the church. Serena and Georgia arrived, and they went over to pay their respects to Owen and Richard.

There were so many relatives that Owen had not seen for years, but he was so pleased that they all found the time to say goodbye to the mum and brother that he loved so deeply. After spending a little time with the relatives, he was able to speak to Serena and Georgia who had been patiently standing to the side out of respect while Owen and Richard were talking to the relatives.

Just as the men were about to speak to Serena and Georgia, Detective Brown, as Brenda liked to call him, walked over to them.

In a quiet voice, he said, 'Good to see you all. How are you doing, Owen?'

Owen replied, 'It's good to see you too, Inspector Brown, I'm so pleased that you could make it.'

'Thank you, Owen. I can't tell you how pleased I am that after all these years Kevin can finally rest in peace with your Mum. What a beautiful ending to such a tragedy I don't think there was a day that went by without me thinking about him, and I thank you so much for inviting me.'

Just then Owen and Richard were asked to get ready for carrying the coffins into the church. Once both coffins were in the church, the service began. Owen had picked his parents' favourite song to be played. It was called 'The beauty of you'. Gavin used to sing it to Brenda before their lives fell apart due to the loss of Kevin, and the nastiness of Catherine Davis, who was adamant on ruining Gavin and his family, and in the end she and her son, succeeded.

The church was packed with mourners and there were still more people who were just neighbours and well-wishers still outside. The service went on for about an hour, and then it came time for everyone to gather around the gravesite.

The people listened to the prayers and the wonderful words that were spoken about both Brenda, and particularly Kevin. There was hardly a dry eye when the priest mentioned how Kevin had been lost in an unknown wilderness until being recovered just weeks ago. Now together again with the parents that had loved and missed him for many years.

As the prayers were being said, Serena looked up to

wipe away her tears and as she did this, she saw movement out of the corner of her eyes.

A short distance away she saw the spirits of Kevin, Brenda and Gavin stood together. This was their way of saying thank you to her for bringing them all back together. She made a slight hand gesture, as if to let them know that she had seen them. They are now at peace.

TOGETHER FOREVER.

The funeral service was now over, and people began to leave except for the ones that had been invited back to the wake, which was in a private room at the pub. When Serena and Georgia arrived, they were invited to sit with Owen and Richard. After about ten minutes Detective Brown approached them.

They all sat chatting for a while when Owen started telling them all about when he was a small child and Kevin his big brother, always looked after him, in his own childlike way. He was always there for him when he fell and hurt himself and was always trying to read him stories from a book that were obviously made up, as Kevin was only about five years old himself, and yet couldn't read properly. Although Kevin had been gone for such a long time now, the love was always there, and will always remain.

Another hour went by, and people were leaving, each of them coming over to Owen to give him their love and condolences. It was soon time for Owen, Richard and the rest of their guests at the table to leave also. Owen invited them all back to the house.

When they arrived, Inspector Brown, who had by now asked them all to call him Arthur, stood and looked at the house that he had been to many times over the years since Kevin had first disappeared, remembering how it looked and how his words that he had to deliver to Brenda and Gavin, time after time, year after year devastated them both.

Arthur found it so surreal being back in the house where there had been so much sadness, remembering the reactions of Brenda and Gavin, but he was glad he was there and that he had made the right decision in going to the funeral.

Then Owen said, 'Arthur, as you know, Serena works trying to help recover cold case victims. Victims like Kevin, who have been missing for decades. She is the one who located Kevin. I'm sorry to have to say this but, the police didn't do enough to find him.'

After all, someone needs to speak for the dead, and that's what people like Serena do.

Arthur turned to look at Richard. 'Yes, you're right about that, even I sometimes think we could do more, but I think it's all to do with government funding, or should I say lack of it, but what they don't realise is that they are literally playing with people's lives.'

Arthur remained friends with them all for five more years, until it was his time to be with his loved ones in the spirit world.

About the Author

E K Alexander emigrated to Australia from England twenty years ago with her husband and five children, all of whom are now grown up and married with children of their own and live happily in this beautiful country. She has been interested in the spiritual side of life for many years and worked as a cold case medium as well as a psychic worker and paranormal investigator. This book has been based on the work she does, and the information received from the spirit world.

Cold Case Medium was written in the hope that people may get to understand that there is more to our life on earth than many of us will ever know or even understand.

Also by E K Alexander

Cold Case Medium
Margaret's Story